# Now I Know Why

## By

## Audre Kramer

© 2001 by Audre Kramer. All rights reserved.

No part of this book may be reproduced, stored in a retrieval system, or transmitted by any means, electronic, mechanical, photocopying, recording, or otherwise, without written permission from the author.

ISBN: 0-7596-7676-3

This book is printed on acid free paper.

1stBooks - rev. 11/27/01

# SKETCHES BY

# CHERI DRAXTEN ANDERSON

# &

# SHIRLEY NOTHNAGEL

## *This Book Is Dedicated To:*

My brother Les, who walked one step ahead of me.

To my husband Michael and my children, Perry, Paige and Mark. They held my hand as I walked through the valley of death.

To my grandchildren: Mollie, Tessa, Madison and Chase. They are the stars that brighten my world.

To my son-in-law, Michael, who encouraged me to learn to use a computer.

# *Contents*

The Early Years .................................................................................. 1

The Willows ...................................................................................... 13

More Hard Times ............................................................................. 29

Beginning Again ............................................................................... 47

Trouble With The P_____ Word ...................................................... 55

Being Jerked Around ........................................................................ 66

Chemo-A Trip To Hell ..................................................................... 75

A Little Bit Of Light ......................................................................... 81

Trouble With The T____ Word ........................................................ 85

Questions Without Answers ............................................................. 91

My Shared NDE ............................................................................... 94

Back To Hell ................................................................................... 101

An Enlightening History ................................................................ 109

Learning "Why" .............................................................................. 115

Joann's Story .................................................................................. 122

Reflections ...................................................................................... 130

## *Introduction*

I write this book with much hesitation. I am not good at crawling out on a limb, but find that is what I must do.

I hope that this book is not your first exposure to Near Death Experience, and I hope it is not your last.

To those who read this book and say "I do not believe it," I reply, "I understand. I lived it and I am still awed by it."

To all skeptics who say "Near Death Experience is not real," I reply "I know for sure that it is."

Though I will always wish I had the traditional type of Near Death Experience, I have to accept the fact that I can not have what I want.

To those who do not believe in God, I can only say that I have no magic words for you. I can only tell you what happened to me.

*Audre Kramer*

*Chapter 1*

# THE EARLY YEARS

This first chapter will consist of many small events designed to give you a glimpse of my childhood. My life began in an old farmhouse in 1943. My parents were quite poor and I was the sixth child born in eight years. We lived near a small town in central Minnesota. Our life was meager to say the least, but as a small child I did not seem to notice.

We lived in an old log structure covered with siding and lined with many layers of lath and wallpaper. The small six-room house did not allow much space for our family of eight plus a hired man. We had a wood stove and minimum electricity but no indoor plumbing.

It was a cold existence in the winter. Sleeping three to a bed helped us keep warm unless the blankets got pulled away. Warm clothes were scarce. We wore hand-me-downs other people had given us. Many were too thin to keep us warm. Mother patched endlessly. My oldest sister, Shirley, learned to sew at age nine or ten. She amazed us with her creations. At that time chicken feed was shipped in cloth sacks. She used these sacks to make shirts, dresses and shorts. With so many of us, we always battled to get the prettiest sack.

One evening Dad was not home and my sister Shirley was sewing with an old treadle machine. She ran the needle through her finger. Mother panicked, as there was no phone or car to get help. My brother ran to a shed to find a pliers to pull the needle out. By the time the extraction was completed everyone was crying, everyone that is, except Shirley. She seemed unusually brave for such a small child.

We were rarely home alone since Dad did not take Mother many places except to church or grocery shopping. She did not know how to drive, nor did she have a car. Most of the time Dad hunted, fished or trapped, and Mom stayed home with us. While home alone, we usually had great adventures. Our ages in 1946 were: Shirley eleven, Bud ten, Lee eight, Elaine six, Les four and I was three.

We did not get much candy; so when we were home alone, we made our own. The trick was to make it, eat it and do the dishes before Mom and Dad got back. Sometimes the candy did not turn out. If we did not boil it long enough the candy did not get hard. Oh well, we ate it anyway. Other times we boiled it too long and it got hard before we got it out of the kettle. Worse yet, sometimes it burned which ruined the flavor, and that did not do much for the kettle either. We dumped the burnt candy down the outdoor toilet hole and scrubbed like the dickens to clean the kettle lest our deed was discovered.

Another time we were half done making the candy and Mother and Dad returned home because the people they intended to visit were gone. We ran out the back door with the kettle and placed it under a tree. The following morning, much to our surprise, some animal licked the pan clean. We think one of Dad's coonhounds profited from our loss.

Most of our mischief seems pretty minor. The boys listened to "Gang Busters" on the radio and that always frightened us littler kids. Other times we took the blankets off the beds and made tents. We spent endless hours sitting on the floor or beds playing cards. Real toys were scarce but we were never bored.

Being home alone had a down side. The hired man liked to go out drinking, and sometimes he returned before Mother and Dad. This was always a frightening situation since he was mean when he was drunk. He drove like a maniac when he came in the yard, and we had to run to get out of the way. When he got out of the car, he staggered so badly that I was afraid he would step on me or kick me. Another time he gave the boys some cheap wine and got them drunk, and he was always after my older sister.

We developed a pretty good defense plan. The first one to see him coming sounded the alarm. Our arsenal of weapons included rocks, homemade slingshots and one precious BB gun shared by Bud and Lee. The boys got his attention while the girls hid. We had many excellent hiding places. One of my favorites was under the granary. There was a small opening in the foundation that I could squeeze through. Other times

*Audre Kramer*

we hid in the hayloft. We tunneled under the hay and were not found. Once my sister, Shirley, was delayed getting under the hay because she hid the smaller kids first. The hired man saw the hay move and started to dig her out. Much to his chagrin Lee popped out of his tunnel and blasted him with the BB gun.

That tactic successfully distracted the hired man and we were safe once more. We were tough little kids and could have passed Survival 101 with ease.

While growing up I hated what drinking did to people. I never lost the fear and disgust I felt during those early incidents. Never developing a desire to drink was the one positive thing to come out of that. Somehow my other siblings seemed to share that feeling, though some of them drank a little socially.

Since we had so few new toys, we had to be very inventive. Dad brought home broken tricycles, scooters, bicycles, wagons and sleds. Being somewhat mechanically inclined, we made usable toys out of the junk. Some of the things we made turned out well, some not so well. We made swings with rotten ropes. When the ropes broke, it was a painful reminder that the ground was hard.

My sisters and I made rag dolls, and we used peach crates for doll beds. We used leftover scraps of cloth from the feed sacks for doll clothes and doll blankets.

Even our pets were freebies. I especially liked baby kittens. There were always stray barn cats around, and I got pretty good at taming them. Also some of Dad's coonhounds would have pups and they were cute when they were little. Sometimes we found baby rabbits in the hay field and tried to raise them. Another time we acquired a lamb, but it was not one of our success stories. It fell down the outdoor toilet hole. We retrieved it from that soupy pit but it did not do too well after that.

Perhaps our greatest accomplishment revolved around a baby Great-Horned owl. It was just a ball of fluff when we found it and we named him Owlie. With some tender loving care it grew to 18" high. My sister Shirley became most familiar with this large owl. Even when we wouldn't see it for days at a time she would call to him with a "screechy" tone and he would fly in and sit on the fence. We marveled at his gyrating head and his blinking double eyelids.

Another time we got some old bedsprings and a mattress. We found some old rope and tied this combination between two trees. That made a swinging hammock big enough to hold all six of us.

One of my earliest memories concern my sister Elaine. My oldest sister Shirley who was involved in the incident and ten years old at the time, best tells this account.

"It was spring, and we raked the lawn and then burned the debris. Mom went inside to start supper, and soon called me to come in and help. My sister Elaine who was five at the time stayed outdoors to play. Mom sent me outside to get a cup of cream from the cooler tank near the well. As I came out the front door, Elaine came running from the lawn area with flames streaming off her back. I grabbed handfuls of sand, trying to throw it on the flames. Immediately I could see that wouldn't work. She headed toward the stock water tank, and I thought to throw her in. Just then, Dad drove in from the field with the tractor and as he rounded the corner he saw Elaine and the flames. He pulled the keys and jumped from the moving tractor. He grabbed Elaine and beat out the flames with his hands. All this took place in less than a minute, from my first glimpse of her until Dad grabbed her.

In retrospect, I probably could not have managed to get her in the water tank considering her size and thrashing about from the pain. She was badly burned as it was. A few more seconds would have been fatal.

Later Elaine told us she had been trying to re-ignite a small pile of smoldering leaves and didn't realize as she squatted down that the hem of her new feed sack dress was touching some ashes behind her.

Years later I saw a movie about pioneers, and a little girl who stayed outside and played with the fire used to cook their meal. She also was badly burned and died. I could not believe how that movie brought back in vivid detail, how terrible that incident was for all of us."

Caring for Elaine under such primitive conditions proved difficult at best. Mom and Dad cleared off the living room table and padded it with blankets. They laid her there on her tummy. Pain control consisted of Shirley fanning her with a newspaper. On the fourth day my uncle and aunt came to visit. Uncle Les was a pharmacist, and he convinced my parents to take her to a doctor. Somehow she survived, but she has some very nasty scars. Even though I was only two and a half years old, I can still remember the smell of the salve used to soothe her burns.

My brother Les, closest to me in age, was four and a half when I was three. I was thin and small for my age and Les was taller and so much stronger. We spent most of our free time together. We climbed most of the trees and buildings on our farm. We spent hours in a broken down Model A, and Les would drive us the places we never got to go.

Sometimes he pulled me around in a wagon he made, and we pretended we were going to visit some imaginary friends named Slees and Swears. When I think back on my life, those days with Les were some of my happiest.

I started first grade at age five. That was such a thrill! I attended a tiny country school just up the road. There were three other kids in my grade. That was my first opportunity to develop my social skills. The other kids were so much fun and learning came easily. However, I also started to notice their nice clothes.

About this time I became aware of the fact that none of us were good criers. I saw other children cry, and it seemed acceptable to other people. We only cried if we got hurt or got licked, and then only for a few minutes. Sometimes I ran and hid to get my crying done. When I got older Mother revealed an incident that occurred before I was born.

Mother was in the front seat of the car, holding my sister who was about a year old. Three older children were in the back seat. My sister cried and fussed while Dad, seated behind the wheel, talked to a friend outside the car. During the conversation Dad became annoyed by the crying. Suddenly he reached over and started hitting the baby. Being very angry, he hit hard enough that Mother held her arms in the way to soften the blows. The message seemed clear. Crying was not well tolerated and risky business. I must have learned not to cry from their example. It seems we all developed the skill of crying on the inside.

At age six I started having more responsibilities. Occasionally I drove a tractor to pick up rocks. I also carried in water from the well or carried in firewood. Mostly, I gathered eggs and wiped dishes. My older brothers and sisters helped Mother milk the cows and feed the pigs and chickens. The boys spent long hours working the fields. The work never ended. At age eight, my oldest sister Shirley did many of the things a mother does. My Mother, a small woman, did many of the things a man does. Dad liked to drive tractors and do occasional welding, but when that was done, he usually went fishing or hunting. His hunting dogs spent as much time in the car as we did. Evidence of that was the dog hair and odor on our clothes after riding in the car. Too many times the dogs did battle with a skunk, and Dad let them back in the car. I was never quite sure; if Dad had to choose between his favorite coonhound and me, just how that would have turned out.

When I was seven, we moved to another farm thirty miles away. The hired man did not move with us since the boys were big enough to do most of the work. What a relief! The new farm had better soil and a better house. This one had indoor water and after a year or so we added an indoor bathroom. This house was much warmer during the winter, and now there were four big bedrooms. Good thing, because another baby was coming.

This pregnancy, my Mother's seventh, was very hard on her. She worked far too hard and became quite ill right after the birth. The boys worked hard to keep up with her outdoor chores. My older sisters cared for Mother, and our new baby brother in addition to all the housework. In a few months my new little brother, Gene, grew big enough for me to take care of. When he started to walk, he went everywhere I went. We had grand times together. We played doctor and hospital. I bandaged him up and put makeshift casts on his arms and legs. It was amazing how he put up with all of that.

While Gene napped, I had some free time. Early one evening I tucked him in for a nap and ran out to play. When I came back a little later, Mother appeared very upset. She said that Dad had whaled on Gene because he was crying while Dad was watching television. The crib and

*Now I Know Why*

the television were both in the living room because the bedroom was being painted. When I looked in the living room, Dad was sitting in his chair watching television, and I could tell he was very angry. Gene was lying in his crib. I could hear a choking, muffled whimper and his crib moved slightly when he made the sound. Unable see his face from where I was standing, I felt too frightened to move closer. I stood there frozen not knowing what to do. I just had to see him. I had to know he was all right. I knew going near the crib would be very risky. Finally, I could not stand it any longer and decided to pretend I needed something from the bedroom. In order to go in there I would pass the crib.

Mustering all my courage I ran through the living room. As I passed the crib, I stopped for an instant. Our eyes met. His little face was dark red from holding back his cries. I ran on and made a clean get away. I felt ashamed of myself. I wanted to grab him and run away.

Gene was a special little brother, and we played together all the time. I read to him and taught him his numbers and the alphabet. He could read and add before he started school.

When I was ten years old, I started a new project. I always wanted a tree house, and I found the perfect tree. Scavenging some boards out of the old corncrib I built a little more each day. Eventually, I added a roof. It was not much to look at but I thoroughly enjoyed playing in it.

One Sunday evening we went to visit our relatives. They lived on a particularly scenic farm. Steep hills, thick woods and rocks galore made it difficult to farm. I always enjoyed playing with my cousin Lois who was a little younger than I. We hiked through the woods and pasture eating nuts and berries as we went. As we sat down to rest, we studied the gravel road that went past their farm.

The road went up a very steep hill. We thought it might be fun to come down that hill on a bicycle. They only had one big bicycle, but we decided both of us could ride on it. We grabbed the bicycle and climbed to the top of the hill. When we looked down that long steep gravel road it was an awesome sight. We both climbed on the bicycle and started down the hill. I was at the handlebars. As we started to gain some speed, it became difficult to maintain our balance. Halfway down we were really truckin' and hit some loose gravel. The bicycle went one way and we went the other. We skidded and rolled through the gravel for what seemed like forever. Finally, we rolled into the ditch and lay there and cried and cried and cried. I think I caught up on some of the crying I had missed in the past years. Gravel was embedded in our skin and hair. Our knees and elbows were raw. After that we both decided to retire from downhill racing.

## *Chapter 2*

# THE WILLOWS

The second summer on our new farm, Les was eleven and I was nine. We were home alone while part of the family attended a wedding and the others worked away from home. One of my older brothers came home to do the milking and noticed one of the milk cows missing. Before he left to return to the wedding he instructed us to go down to the first pasture and look for the cow. "Do not cross the river and do not go into the willows," he warned. "Remember what happened to us last summer."

The warning brought back the memories of Bud and Lee being lost in the willows the first summer we moved to the new farm. The willows, a large area of trees and tall brush, was a damp and boggy area. The cows loved to wander through it. The cows walked single file, forming narrow paths everywhere. Bud and Lee begun searching for the cows early one evening and were caught deep in the willows after dark. When they did not return home we called the neighbors and began a search. It took several vehicles with bright lights and loud horns to lead them out.

We listened to the instructions and headed down the long lane leading to the first pasture. Being barefoot as usual the soles of our feet were tough as leather. Since it was early in the evening we thought we had plenty of time. We tramped leisurely through the three mud holes in the lane and strolled into the pasture. After checking all the likely spots, we determined the cow must be across the river.

Walking up to the bank, we surveyed the river. The area where the cows crossed was not usually very deep. Les stuck his foot in the water saying, "Well it's nice and warm. I think we can make it across. I bet that darn cow is just behind that hill. Let's try it. If it gets too deep, we'll just go back." Slowly we waded in. Halfway across, the water rose above my waist with the current pulling at my legs. "How much deeper will it get?" I asked. Les replied, "Probably just a couple more inches. Give me your hand and hold on. I'll be one step ahead of you. Don't be afraid." The water rose to my chest and I felt relieved when we reached the bank. We did not mind our wet clothes. They could dry on the way back home.

We climbed the hill, checking everywhere except the willows. No cow in sight! "Hey, would you like to see a pile of old bones over by the fence line?" Les asked. "Yeah, I'd like to see that," I replied. As we traveled in that direction we nearly walked into a paper wasp nest attached to some brush next to the path. We stopped just in time and went around it. "We'll have to remember where that nest is and come back and torch it next time we come down here," Les said.

We found the bone pile. After examining the skull, we decided it must have been a horse. Some of the bones were huge. All of them were porous. We figured the bones had been there for a long time.

*Now I Know Why*

By this time we were sure that darn cow was hiding in the willows. Where else could it be? Les studied the sky to tell the time. It seemed so bright we thought darkness was a long way off.

Les said, "I've been in there in the daytime with Bud and Lee. We could go in a little way and holler for it. Maybe it'll come out. As long as it doesn't get dark, we'll be fine." It seemed like a good idea. Somewhere along the line we conveniently forgot the earlier warning.

We entered the willows through one of the narrow openings. The paths were so much different than the ones in the pasture. These circled constantly, branching in different directions every hundred feet or so. The bogs made walking difficult, but if we looked where we stepped it went pretty good. We hollered as we walked but still no cow. "Well, I give up," Les said, "we better turn around and go back."

The thick willows formed a tight canopy overhead, greatly reducing the light. That prevented us from seeing any landmarks.

We followed the path back but it did not lead us out. "I can't figure this out," Les said, "we should be out by now." In a few minutes time the light began to fade. "Oh oh, it's later than I thought," Les said. We started to run but found we were being swallowed up by darkness. We lost the last bit of light that filtered through the trees. The path disappeared in front of us and so did our hands and feet. The branches scratched our skin as we moved. We found ourselves totally consumed by the darkness. We became separated right away. We both stopped and called to each other until we touched. We realized we were hopelessly "lost" and no one was home to come looking for us.

Nervously Les said, "give me your hand. We have to stay together. I'll be one step ahead of you. We'll be all right." That was a tall order for an eleven year old boy.

We moved much slower now, stumbling on the bogs and tree roots. Our bare feet took a beating and the mosquitoes feasted on our bare skin. We put our arms up and ahead of us to shield our faces from the branches. We walked a long time and barely spoke.

Suddenly Les stopped. We pulled close to each other. "Do you hear it?" he whispered. I waited. Then, there it was. Something was moving off to the left! Then it stopped too. "Don't move," he whispered, "maybe it'll go away." "What is it?" I asked. "I don't know, but it's not the cow. They don't sound like that when they walk," he replied. "It might be a deer." We could not bear to think it was anything else. A deer was just fine with us. Slowly we began to move again.

During the next half hour our ordeal continued. Several times we heard movement around us. Hoping there were a lot of deer in there, we tried to concentrate on finding a way out. Neither of us cried or complained though we were both terrified.

More time passed and we became exhausted. Each step hurt our sore feet. Suddenly Les cried out, "Ouch! I hit something sharp and it stuck me." Carefully he felt in front of him. It was a barbed wire fence. He said, "We must have walked all the way through the willows. I'm so tired, let's rest a minute."

As we rested I became more frightened. Would we ever find our way out? All at once Les was on his feet. He said, "I know how to get out of here. We'll follow the fence. It should lead us to the river and we'll follow it to the cattle crossing."

We felt rejuvenated and ready to move. Holding on to the barbed wire hurt our hands, but we did not seem to notice. At last we walked in a straight line instead of around in circles. It took a long time to reach the river, but when we finally did we got our first glimpse of moonlight on the water. It was beautiful.

Following the riverbank proved tricky. It was overgrown and the water would have been deep if we slipped in. After a considerable struggle we found the cattle crossing. However, crossing the river at night frightened me. I hesitated, but not for long. Les grabbed my hand and started across. "I'll hold on to you and stay one step ahead. Don't be afraid," he said. The water felt good on our sore feet. We struggled with the current and the darkness. Finally, we made it safely across, sure now the worst was behind us. We lay on the shore to rest since we still were one half mile from home. Suddenly we could hear movement on the bank several feet above us. "What was that?" I asked Les. "I'm almost too tired to care," he replied. A few seconds later we heard it again. We decided to investigate and slowly crept up the bank. Cautiously we peered over the edge. Sure enough there was a large black form standing just a few feet away! It was that darn cow. "Well," Les said, "we flushed her out of the willows after all." Now we'd better get her home." We felt like tying a knot in her tail, but we did not have the energy. It was time to get moving. Maybe we could get home before anyone missed us.

We ran up the lane chasing the cow ahead of us. Our feet were in terrible condition. We decided to wear our shoes for a few days so no one would notice the cuts on our feet. As we neared the barn it was plain to see, someone was home. The lights were on in the house.

"We better make up a story pretty quick or we'll be in trouble," Les said. We stumbled through the door to meet Dad in the kitchen. "Where the hell have you two been? We've been home fifteen minutes and hollered for you and you didn't answer. How come you're all wet?" he snorted. Les replied, "Oh we were just playing hide-and-go-seek and we had a little fun with the water hose earlier. "Well, get to bed right now and I don't want to hear a peep out of you," he ordered. Well, we went to bed and we did not peep.

Years later when Bud and Lee talked about their ordeal in the willows at age thirteen and fifteen, Les and I kept our secret.

Milking was a big job on our farm. We did a lot of things by hand. Mother and the boys did an excellent job. That milk check fed and clothed us. Dad disliked cows and usually was not around when it was time to milk.

One evening while Mother and the boys were milking, Dad was in the barn skinning some critter he trapped that day. A calf had just been born and Mother tried to help it start to nurse from the cow. The nervous cow did not stand still to allow the weak calf to suck. Mother was not having much success. Dad got angry and ordered Mother to the house. When she came in, she was upset and said that Dad was going to teach that calf to suck or else. I put on my coat and ran to the barn. I wish I would not have. When I got near the mother cow I saw a bloody milk stool he used to persuade the calf. He was holding the calf up by its hind legs. He had used his skinning knife to cut its throat. Later one of my brothers told Mother they did not want Dad in the barn when they were milking.

When I reflect on this incident, I know it is part of the reason, I am still frightened when Dad gets angry.

When Les and I got home from school, we had chores to do. If I got done first, sometimes I helped him. I either helped him feed the cows or climbed the silo with him and threw down the silage. That is, if the silo was not so full that I had to climb to the top. Early in the autumn, the silo was full, and later in the winter and early spring it was lower so I did not mind climbing it. I was an accomplished climber since Les and I had done it all through our childhood. If we got bored, we just found something to climb. There was nary a tree or building on our farm that we had not climbed one time or another. However, the top of the silo was something else. I only climbed it once and I decided that was enough.

At age fourteen and a half, Les and mother did most of the barn chores. Bud and Lee had grown up and had jobs of their own. After school, Les and I came home and went to work. One afternoon when Les came home, he felt unusually tired. He lay down for what he thought would be just a few minutes. I started my chores and forgot about him. Mom, busy with her chores, did not realize Les had not gone out to the barn. About an hour later, I finished hauling in wood and went to watch TV. Suddenly I realized Les was still asleep. I ran up to his room to wake him. He had fallen into a deep sleep. As he was waking up, it was obvious that he was not feeling well. Sitting on the edge of his bed, he looked out the window, he was dismayed to see that it was nearly dark. "Oh no," he said, "it is almost dark. How am I going to throw down the silage in the dark? I can't do all the chores alone. You have to help me." Looking at his pale face, I knew he needed some help. I agreed.

We scrambled down the stairs and got dressed. Then I remembered. The silo was filled a few weeks earlier. That meant we had to climb to the top. I did not like climbing it in the daylight, and doing it in the dark terrified me. I wanted to back out of my commitment, and said to Les, "We can't climb that silo now. It will be pitch dark in there. Maybe we should feed the cows extra hay and forget about the silage." He replied, "We can't do that. The cows will go down on milk if we try that. We'll use Dad's big flashlight and we'll be able to see just fine." I went to the cabinet where Dad kept his flashlight on the top shelf. I pulled open the door. To my dismay the light was not there. Then I remembered, Dad had gone coon hunting. He took the light with him. "What are we going to do now?" I asked. "Don't worry," Les replied, "I'll make us a flashlight out of the old broken ones left in the drawer." As I finished putting on some warm clothes, I could hear Les rummaging through the drawers. "Come on, come on, you bugger, light up!" He sounded desperate. Abruptly his tone changed. "I got it, I got it," he shouted, "this one works! It's not great, but I think it will last long enough to get us through. Let's get going."

We headed out the door into the darkness, breathing the cold, crisp air. As we entered the barn I could smell the moist odor that is always present during the winter months. We went directly to the silo room and prepared

*Now I Know Why*

for the long climb ahead of us. Our silo was taller than the barn. A metal chute, about three feet in diameter, ran up the side of the silo. Inside the chute was a metal ladder. I really did not want to do this, but before I could think of a way to back out, Les said, "I'll go first. I will attach the loop on the end of the flashlight to the snap on my coat so that it will shine down toward you. Stay right behind me and you'll be fine."

He entered the chute, waiting for me to follow. With the dim light I could barely make out the ladder well enough to see where to grab. The chute and the ladder were slippery and covered with frost which forms as the silage passes through it. I tried to focus upward and climb as fast as Les, in an effort to forget about where I was and how high I was climbing. As Les climbed, the flashlight kept flickering off and on. I asked him what was wrong with it? He replied that it was just a poor contact and would stop flickering when he could stop moving.

The chute made our voices sound hollow and there was a slight echo effect as we climbed higher. About half way up, I became somewhat fearful, and grasped the ladder more tightly as I climbed. A little farther up, I felt much more uncomfortable. I wished I was somewhere else. I knew I had to forget about where I was and focus on what I must do. A fall from this height meant certain death, or at least horrible injury. I did not want either one, so I decided I must pay attention to the ladder and forget about everything else.

Finally, Les said, "This is it! I've reached the opening (narrow, thirty inches in diameter). I will crawl through and help you get inside." As he moved, the light went with him. I climbed up to the opening, and Les grabbed my arm and pulled me in. It was awesome. The dome of the silo was just above us. It made me realize how high we had climbed. For a moment I felt a little light-headed, which was ridiculous since there was plenty of air in there. I disliked the sour fermented smell of the silage that filled the air. It always amazed me what a little time would do to corn stalks after it is chopped into small pieces and stored in a silo. I could never understand how the cows could eat that stuff without getting sick.

Les propped up the flashlight with a clump of silage, and it stopped flickering. He grabbed the silage fork and said, "We'd better move pretty fast. That light won't last forever." I agreed, since it barely cast a dim glow around us. A fork full of silage landed on my boots. I grabbed the other fork and started to throw some silage down the chute. As it fell, it thundered down the chute. I could hear silage bouncing off the ladder and the sides of the chute. It finally made a barely audible splattering sound on the floor below.

Using our usual system Les went to the middle of the silo and threw the silage toward the opening. I stood by the opening and threw the silage into the chute. We worked extremely fast and spoke very little. In the past part of my job was to look down the chute and make sure that we did not throw down too much silage. That would plug the bottom of the chute making it impossible for us to get back out. Suddenly I realized I could not see down the chute because of the darkness. I asked Les, "How will we know when we've thrown down enough silage?" He replied, "When you're up this high you can't really see to the bottom even when it's light outside. I think I'll be able to tell when it's enough because I've done it so many times."

*Now I Know Why*

We worked at a feverish pace. As the light grew slowly dimmer we worked faster yet. I started to get warm and sweaty, but did not bother to open my coat. I did not want to waste the time. A few more minutes passed and the light went out and came back on. This time there was barely a glow left. Les threw his fork down and said, "Come on, we're getting out of here! You shine the light into the chute while I climb out. When I get out there, hand the light to me, and I will shine it toward you." The most frightening part of this ordeal was crawling through the narrow opening and into the chute. This maneuver could easily cause a nasty fall.

As I handed the light to Les, it went out again. This time shaking it did not make it come back on. We were in total darkness! I was terribly frightened. How could I get into the chute without a light to see what I was doing? "Les, are you there?" I said with a shaky voice. "I'm right here," he replied, "don't be afraid, I'll help you get out. Put your foot through the opening. I will grab it and put it on the ladder." That went pretty well. Then he said, "Put your arm through the opening and try to feel the ladder." Carefully I groped around and found the ladder. I took a firm grip, and swung my body through the opening into the chute. Les still had a hold of my leg and he said, "We'll have to come down slowly and carefully. If you fall, I won't be able to hold both of us up." Slowly, we began the descent. We had to feel around with our hands and feet to find the steps before we could let go of the step we were holding onto. The darkness, the cold, the slippery ladder and our fear made the climb seem endless. It seemed a painfully slow procedure, but with each step we were that much closer to the bottom. Half way down I felt something crunch beneath my boot. Les shouted, "Hey, slow down up there! You just stepped on my fingers!" "Are you all right?" I asked, "I didn't mean to do it. I can't see a darn thing." He replied, "Yeah, I'm all right. I have my gloves on. It didn't hurt too much."

I began to descend more slowly, and put down my feet more carefully. I knew we must be getting close to the bottom so I was not quite so frightened. A few steps later, Les shouted, "Stop! Don't come down any further. I'm standing on silage. I guess we threw down more than I thought because the chute is plugged. Climb up a few steps so I have some room to jump and kick. I think I can pack it down enough to cause an opening. If not, we'll have to wait until Mom misses us for supper and comes looking for us. She'll be able to dig us out." I climbed back up and waited. After jumping just a few times Les shouted, "My boot slid through. I can dig us out of here." A few minutes later we were free and extremely exhausted. We went to the house for a quick supper. Les was feeling quite sick by then so Mom and I helped him milk the cows and finish the chores.

After climbing the silo that night, I seemed to lose my interest in climbing. I preferred to keep at least one foot on the ground. I guess that was all right. I was growing up and seemed to be interested in other things.

I attended a small country school through the eighth grade. I loved country school. It was so much fun and no one seemed to care about my less than fashionable wardrobe.

Ninth grade in a city school was a rude awakening. I was tall and skinny (5'7", 110 lbs.), and my clothes were terrible. I was not accustomed to homework either. The extra studying to hold onto my good grades strained my eyes. My glasses began to grow in thickness. That was miserable. I got teased enough to know that I never wanted to hurt someone else that way. I could not ask for new clothes.

My brothers never got to go to high school. They had to stay home and work on the farm. I became keenly aware of that one morning around the time Les should have entered the tenth grade, but could not. He was luckier than Bud and Lee. They had to quit after the eighth grade.

One morning Mother came in from the barn very upset because Dad and Les were having an argument. I hated seeing her like that because it always frightened me. I glanced out the window and saw Dad drive away. That meant it was safe to run to the barn and check on Les.

As I came through the barn door, Les was hard at work cleaning a thick layer of manure from the calf pens. When he saw me, he quickly wiped his tears, smearing his face badly because his hands were dirty. He did not say anything, but I could tell he was angry. He jabbed the fork deep into the manure and threw it as far as he could. I pretended to be looking for one of the cats and kicked around the straw while observing him. Being embarrassed by his tears he did not want to talk. It was one of the few times I ever saw him cry. After a while I returned to the house. I never knew what they argued about. Maybe it was school or maybe he was fed up with Dad's system of putting everyone to work and then taking off.

A few months later it was cultivating time and Les and Dad were at it from sunup to sundown. Each morning Dad and Les checked the cultivator settings to be sure they were not out of adjustment. Dad always double-checked Les's cultivator after he was done adjusting his. When Les finished, he jumped on his tractor and headed for the field. As he drove past, Dad yelled, "Hey come back here. I haven't checked your cultivator yet." Les shouted back, "That's all right, I haven't checked yours either." He kept right on going. It took Dad quite awhile to see the humor in that one. Les was a super mechanic and after that, Dad found himself asking Les for mechanical advice on a regular basis.

At fourteen my life got a little more complicated. I was invited on a hayride one autumn evening with a group of friends. During the ride I was sitting on the edge of the rack and got knocked off. I hit my head on the gravel and fell unconscious for a brief period. When I woke-up, I felt a little embarrassed and was anxious to get back on the rack. Later when I got home I realized that I was injured. My neck felt very painful and my vision seemed affected. The following day Mom took me to a doctor. He diagnosed torn ligaments in my neck. Now I had a steel neck brace to add to my wardrobe. I wore the brace for two weeks then the doctor decided my injury had healed. That seemed too good to be true.

Six months later my neck felt so weak it became difficult to hold my head up. We returned to the doctor and learned that the muscle tissue on the injured side of my neck had shrunk. It seems there was a hairline fracture of the vertebrae that went undetected. It took over a year of physical therapy and very restricted activity for it to heal permanently. What a drag. Oh well, it could have been worse. I could have been paralyzed.

I really needed money to improve my appearance. Getting a summer job at a drive-in I saved everything I earned. When school started in the fall I had better clothes. I found another job after school and kept working. By now my glasses were really thick. No matter what frame I picked I still did not look good. Contact lenses were just coming on the market and were very expensive. I saved until I had enough to buy a pair. That seemed so much better.

Next I needed to see a dentist. My teeth were long overdue for some work. Saving again I finally got them taken care of. All of these needs kept me very busy. I was either working or studying. I missed all the football and basketball games that other kids took for granted. Sometimes I wondered what that would have been like to do just a few of those things. At least I was allowed to go to school, and I made some really good friends.

As graduation grew near, I decided to go on to college and become a registered nurse. I applied at the St. Cloud School of Nursing. My grades were good and I passed the entrance exams. I made one big mistake when I filled in the registration forms. They inquired about my physical condition. I was truthful and explained my neck injury which was nearly healed. They rejected me. Their philosophy was that to be an RN you needed a strong spine in order to lift patients. Starting out with a weak neck would only lead to further back problems. When I discussed this with my school counselor, he advised me to lie about my injury in the

*Audre Kramer*

future. I was really disappointed. I did not want to lie, yet I wanted be a nurse. I decided to work a year and try again after my injury completely healed.

*Chapter 3*

# MORE HARD TIMES

My life took a different direction. Rather than going on to college, I used my math and accuracy skills to start a brief career as a bookkeeper. I enjoyed this type of work and let college slip away. I also met Ron, a hardworking, handsome guy three years older than myself. We seemed to really hit it off. He seemed very quiet around other people but talkative and friendly when we were alone. He seemed kind and gentle, two extremely important qualities I wanted in a husband. We dated for two years. During that time we were around his family very little. Alcoholism appeared to be a serious problem with them and he knew I didn't tolerate that kind of behavior very well.

As we grew closer to marriage I asked him several times if he had a problem with giving up alcohol. He always replied that he did not. The last time we discussed it he seemed hurt and replied, "Do you think I want to be like them?" We did not discuss it again.

*Audre Kramer*

We planned to be married in the spring and I felt confident I had made a good choice. Our marriage classes were nearly completed and the wedding plans progressed smoothly.

Our tiny country church had no resident pastor; however, a priest from a neighboring parish came each Sunday for one service. The neighboring parish actually had two priests. Father B, a young man just out of the seminary and Father C, an experienced, middle aged man. Each Sunday they alternated, and we always made our wedding plans with Father B, who appeared very friendly and greeted us with a smile. Father C seemed to resent assisting with our parish. He usually seemed cranky and always preached about money, something our little parish lacked.

A few weeks before the wedding Father C was saying Mass and near the end, he made the following announcement. "If anyone here knows Audre Nothnagel, please tell her to call me right away, or there just will not be a wedding." I was not present but my family was, and they were very embarrassed. He made it sound like we had done something terribly wrong.

Ron and I went to see Father C that same afternoon. We were dismayed to learn that all he wanted was the letter stating that we had completed our marriage classes. Father B already had this information. We could not understand why he did not simply call us on the phone instead of dropping that little bomb in front of the whole congregation. He seemed so cranky, we were afraid to ask. We decided to go to great lengths to avoid him in the future.

After the wedding and a short honeymoon, we settled into a cheap crummy apartment. It had not been lived in for several years and it had a

*Now I Know Why*

foul musty odor. We scrubbed and painted and were amazed at how nice it turned out. We had a nice cozy place to live with plenty of room.

About the tenth day of our marriage I was in for a real shock. We were alone in our apartment and all at once Ron changed. It was sudden and unexpected with no logic or reason. He started to tease and make fun of me. He said I had a crummy job and must be stupid to work there. He kept on and on with anything he could think of until I started to cry. Then he laughed at me. After about an hour he changed back to normal. I reminded myself that we dated two whole years and I never saw this type of behavior. I thought it was just a bad mood and would probably never happen again.

As time went on, these episodes did occur again, about every two or three weeks. I could not understand how he could do that if he loved me. After the third time I could not stand to see him laugh when I cried. I vowed that he would never make me cry again. As a child, I learned crying was risky business. This was even worse. Crying was definitely not for me. It always made things worse. I would have to be good at crying on the inside.

I wanted to be just as tough as he was, so I tried every approach I could think of to cope with it. I tried begging, talking, threats and just plain ignoring him but nothing reached him. During these episodes he appeared completely unrational, but it always did pass. I kept telling myself that somehow we could lick this thing.

About two months into the marriage it became obvious to me that his family's alcohol problems were becoming our problems. Ron demanded we spend more time with his family. Ron's mother always encouraged him to drink. She knew I did not want him to drink more than a few bottles at a time. She poured her beer into his bottle when I was not looking. That way I could not tell how much he drank. She had a steady supply to keep this little charade going.

As we spent more time with Ron's family, I began to study his family's behavior patterns. On Friday evening his parents started drinking. It continued all day Saturday and Sunday. His mother drank more than his father and she became more out of control than his Father. In the bars he struggled to keep track of her.

One evening we were driving home after a particularly disturbing weekend with Ron's family. He revealed to me what it was like when he was a small child. He said, "My parents came home from the bars late at night. They were always drunk and got into a loud fight. I heard them knocking things over and sometimes they hit each other. All of us kids woke up and were so frightened. Since I was the oldest (eventually there were ten children) they came running into my bed, and I had to take care of them and keep them quiet."

Later, I thought about Ron's childhood. It was his job to comfort his younger brothers and sisters when they were frightened, and there was no one to comfort Ron. He was just a young child himself, probably six or seven years old. I learned the drinking had been there from the beginning and wondered what else he could remember before the age of six.

I soon discovered every holiday was the same. Their drinking ruined every event. The smaller children poured the booze down the drain every chance they had. However, some of the older children stole it and drank it themselves.

After five months of marriage and the Catholic rhythm method for birth control, I became pregnant. I loved children and hoped this would help Ron grow up. In some ways I think it made a difference. There were still disturbing incidents that were always connected to his mother, but there were also times when I really believed he was gaining an edge. However, maybe I was just fooling myself. Now I was pregnant and that would be difficult to handle alone. I remembered my strict Catholic teachings. Divorce was a no-no or at best a shameful thing.

Our friends Jerry and Karen were expecting a baby about the same time as Ron and I. This was the second child for them so it was fun to visit with them and discuss our future arrivals. Sometimes we get together after Mass on Sunday. We would have lunch and play cards all afternoon.

One Sunday when we attended Mass, it was Father C's turn at our parish. He seemed his usual grumpy self. While he was giving his sermon, Jerry and Karen's eighteen-month-old child started to fuss. When they did not leave fast enough to suit Father C, he asked them to take the child out. They did, and they never attended Mass there again. Father C struck again!

Time for the big event drew near and I became enormous. My sisters teased me because I was always so skinny and now I looked liked an orange with toothpicks for arms and legs. It didn't concern me too much until I passed my due date. Each morning when I woke up still pregnant, I felt like crying. I theorized that most babies were born at night and I had another whole day of waiting. Another whole day of gaining weight; another whole day of my baby getting bigger. I was one week overdue and still, no baby. Now I felt a little scared! What could be wrong?

Finally, on the morning of the eleventh day I woke up at six o'clock am feeling lousy. I became exhausted walking from the bedroom to the bathroom and then I felt some cramps. They were mild, but I was sure today was going to be the day. Ron had left for work but would be off at noon. That seemed perfect. I was ready to go to the hospital when he got home.

After being admitted and prepped, the contractions felt much stronger. My doctor examined me and said my delivery was several hours away. He left the hospital after telling the nurses how he could be reached.

During the afternoon, time moved very slowly. The contractions felt strong and seemed closer together. I clung to my doctor's remark of "several more hours." I could manage that even though I became more exhausted as each hour passed.

Finally, at six o'clock, and my doctor came in to check me . "Well, he said, "you haven't dilated very far considering the strength of your contractions. I think your baby is fairly big so I guess this will take a little longer." I asked him for something for the pain and he said that it was too risky for the baby.

I felt crushed! I wanted to get this over with. How could I stand more of this pain? And I was so tired! The nurses seemed concerned and sympathetic. They were in and out of my room more frequently now. As the contractions grew worse they pulled up the sides of my bed to keep me from rolling off. One nurse gave me her hand to hold, but she only did it once. I squeezed it so hard I hurt her. I held onto the railings of my bed when the contractions came. Other times I grabbed the head of the bed and pushed to gain some leverage. Ron stayed by my side and the look on his face reflected the fear he felt.

Eight o'clock came and went. I had dilated to four or five, but it was still a long way to ten. The contractions felt like a knife twisting in my back, and now they were closer together and lasting much longer. Breathing became difficult to accomplish during such intense pain.

Nine o'clock, ten o'clock, eleven o'clock, eleven thirty; I had only dilated to six. Finally, the doctor took Ron out in the hall for a conference. He said, "Something is wrong! I believe the baby is coming backwards and it is pretty big. We are running out of time. Your wife is too exhausted to last much longer and it is too late to turn the baby around. I'm going to give her a shot to slow the contractions. Maybe if she can rest for a few minutes, she will be able to push harder. If that doesn't work, I will need your permission to do a cesarean section. I must tell you at this stage, it will be very difficult to stop the contractions long enough to remove the baby. It will be extremely risky." Feeling he didn't have any other options, Ron gave his consent.

The doctor returned to my room and explained the procedure. I could barely understand what he said. They gave me an injection and fell into a subconscious state. The contractions lightened up for about ten minutes then returned with a vengeance. Soon I could feel the pressure of the baby moving down. The nurses quickly summoned the doctor and confirmed that it was time to move to the delivery room. It was immediately obvious the baby was a boy. He was coming butt first.

Ron was not allowed in the delivery room. The pace in there seemed much faster as the nurses scurried around to get the equipment in place.

*Audre Kramer*

The doctor said, "You will feel some sharp sticks as I inject you with the novacaine. I'm going to give you extra shots to make this more comfortable." When I saw the length of the needle I knew it would hurt. But then, everything hurt.

Finally, Perry arrived! I felt too weak to hold him and I only got a quick look at him before the nurses whisked him away. As I lay on the table I could see the doctor sewing me up. With each stitch I saw him lift the needle high in the air. The string was very long. I got the idea there were many stitches. Shortly thereafter, I slipped into a deep sleep.

The next thing I remember, a terrible pain in my arm pulled me to a conscious state. In the dimly lit room, I did not know where I was or what caused the pain. I saw a nurse at my side. She did something and muttered to herself. The pain in my arm returned and I knew she caused it. She said, "This can't be right." She left the room and I started to slip away again. The pain returned and when I opened my eyes there were two nurses at my side. They had something wrapped around my arm that made it hurt, and I groaned. One of the nurses said, "I'm sorry we are hurting you. Your arms are very sore from pulling on the bed during your long labor and delivery. Your blood pressure has dropped very low, and we must check it often. Try to sleep and don't be afraid, we will take good care of you." I slipped away again.

Later, I awoke again. My arm still hurt, but there was no one in the room. As I looked around I saw something laying on my arm. Why would they lay something on my sore arm? It was covered with a blanket, and I thought, "This must be a baby. Why would they bring me a baby?" Then, slowly, I started to remember; "I think I had a baby! Yes, I'm sure I had a baby. This must be my baby!" I wanted to see him. I pulled the blanket away, but I could only see the top of his head. I had to lift my head in order to see his face and hands. When I tried to do that I realized how weak I was and how painful it was to move. Resting a minute I tried again. This time I got a quick glimpse of his face. He was beautiful, and he was mine! I wanted to hold him and cuddle him, but I could not. My arm throbbed where his head rested. Reluctantly, I slipped my arm from under his head and cuddled him by laying my arm along his side. I found his hands and touched his tiny fingers. I felt exhilarated but struggled to stay awake. Soon a nurse came and took him away. I could hardly wait to wake up again so I could see him.

By the next day I began to understand what happened to me. There were many other mothers in the maternity ward and they were able to walk. When it was time for me to walk, I needed a nurse on each side of me, and I still could not stand up. Most of the other mothers could sit. I could not. Even lying down caused my stitches to hurt. The other mothers had some discomfort; my entire body ached.

When my doctor made his morning rounds, he explained what had happened. He said, "You had a large baby, almost nine pounds. He was born in the breech position, that is, butt first with his legs under his tummy. That is why you had such a long and difficult delivery and that is why you are so weak. When your baby was born, I cut you as far as I could but it was not enough, and you tore quite a bit. I want you to know that I have repaired all the damage and eventually you will be fine. You will need mechanical assistance with some of your bodily functions for awhile so you will not leave the hospital as soon as some of the other mothers." Before the doctor left the room I asked him, "How many stitches do I have?" He replied, "You have enough."

It was common practice at that time to have babies baptized as soon as possible, usually within a week. The Catholic Church taught that if a baby died before being baptized it could not go to heaven. It was not possible to have Perry baptized that first Sunday, since I stayed in the hospital for a week. However, on Sunday Ron went to see Father B to make the arrangements to have Perry baptized. He said he would be happy to do it the following Sunday right after Mass which was his turn to be at our parish. My mother volunteered to host the celebration afterward since I still could not sit. I either had to stand or lie down. With the sponsors at hand we arrived at the church at the appropriate time. Much to our surprise, Father C. abruptly met us at the door. He stated he would not baptize Perry because we were no longer members of the parish. We were dumbfounded! We asked, "What do you mean?" "We have always attended this church." He snorted, "After you got married, you moved to Litchfield. That is not my district. You will have to get a release from the priest in Litchfield before I will baptize your baby." We responded, "It is too late to do that today, and the sponsors have traveled a long way, and the food is all prepared for the dinner." It did not matter. It seemed clear by the look on his face, he would have gladly argued the point. It was useless. We became angry and walked away from the church.

When I got to the car I was so upset I forgot about my stitches and sat on the car seat. Darn, that really hurt! On the way back to Litchfield, I lay

*Now I Know Why*

in the back seat with Perry beside me. With Ron at the wheel he said, "Someone has got to teach this guy how to use a phone. I wish Father B would have tipped us off."

We drove directly to the rectory of the priest in Litchfield. We explained the events to him and he replied, "Well, I'll give you a release right now. It doesn't matter to me where you get your baby baptized." We thought for a moment, and replied, "Father, will you baptize our baby? We are so angry with Father C that we don't want him near our baby." He replied, "I can't do it today because I have other commitments, but I will be glad to do it next Sunday." We agreed. The following Sunday the sponsors returned, the meal was prepared again, and Perry was baptized at the ripe old age of three weeks. And I could finally sit!

After this we realized we could not attend Mass and think one Godly thought while looking at Father C's miserable unloving face. It was a rude awakening to me to realize a priest and God are definitely not the same. (I was a little slow figuring out Santa Claus, too.) We decided to attend Mass at our parish only when Father B presided. We attended Mass elsewhere when it was Father C's presided. Shortly thereafter, another nice priest was assigned to our parish full time, and we greatly appreciated having him.

It felt great having my own little baby. I loved rocking him, holding him and just watching him sleep. Wandering back into my childhood I could not remember being held or cuddled by my parents. I remembered being rocked by my sister, Shirley, when I had an earache. Another time my sister, Elaine, carried me to the house after I slashed my head on an iron bar in the barn. I wanted Perry's childhood to be better than mine. This was going to be an important job.

Ron got a new job. It was the beginning of his truck driving career. He appeared to be good at it and he learned the techniques much faster than the other new drivers. It also kept him away from home a lot. When home he slept a good deal to compensate for the sleep he missed on the road. Things seemed quieter since there was less time for us to be together and less time spent with his parents.

By now it was time for my younger brother, Gene, (who learned so quickly he had skipped the third grade) to enter high school. All my brothers and sisters got together and made it clear to Dad that Gene was going to high school. It was useless for him to object; we were older now and a force to be reckoned with. Dad gave in and Gene was on his way. He was the only one of my brothers who was allowed to graduate from high school. Not only that, he went on to college at the University of Minnesota and earned a bachelor's degree in physics and math; then on to the University of Southern Illinois for a master's degree in art and physics. Then to Cornell University in New York for another master's degree and a PHD in applied physics. Currently, he is a professor at the University of California. I think that is just grand! I am so proud of him and of my other brothers and sisters who went on to build good lives in spite of our difficult beginnings.

*Now I Know Why*

When we grew up, we each got married and became good loving parents. Shirley worked with a show business troupe for a short time before her children were born and later went into real estate. Bud owns an auto sales business. Lee owns an auto repair business. Elaine went to college and became an elementary teacher. Les became a successful farmer and owned a trucking business.

*   *   *

The next two years of my life were more of the same. Contact with Ron's family meant more bad moods. I suspected the moods were definite temporary personality changes. Still I hoped, the longer we were married, somehow these personalities would fade.

Near the end of 1966 I became pregnant again. I definitely wanted another child someday and Ron seemed happy about it. I observed Ron trying hard to be a good father to Perry and I felt some degree of confidence he would succeed.

I decided to choose a different doctor for this pregnancy. I felt the other doctor was not observant enough and let things go too far before he interceded. This time I did my homework and made a more careful selection.

My pregnancy went fairly well, but as I grew closer to my due date I became concerned about the delivery. I became enormous again. The doctor thought I would have another large baby. One week before my due date I had another checkup. I discussed with my doctor the possibility of an induced labor if we could determine beforehand the baby was positioned with its head down. He said he would consider it and we would discuss it again on my due date.

The following week I returned for another checkup and I reminded my doctor about our earlier discussion. He did a thorough examination and thought for a moment. "Well, he began, you are carrying a large baby, and its head is down right now. If it turns, I'm not sure you could deliver it. I think we should have a birthday party tomorrow morning. Can you be at the hospital by seven?" My reply was instantaneous. I felt so relieved!

The following morning, May 18, 1967, I entered the hospital and the procedure went smoothly. After being induced Paige was born two and a half hours later. Much different than the eighteen hours I endured when Perry was born. The doctor was right, Paige was a large baby, well over nine pounds. This time I could hold my baby right away, and I felt strong enough to spend several hours getting acquainted with her. I felt so happy! I had a wonderful three year old son and a beautiful baby daughter.

Paige seemed colicky and we spent a good deal of time in the rocking chair. That greatly reduced the time I spent with Perry. I felt concerned he would resent this, but somehow he thought she was just grand. He loved her right away. It was so much fun to watch him play with her. As they grew older their attachment remained strong. When we rode in the car she always used Perry's shoulder for her pillow. That bond proved valuable during the difficult years ahead.

When Paige was two months old, an incident occurred which really upset me. I went shopping and left Ron to care for Perry (three years old) and Paige. When I came home Perry looked upset. Ron told me he had played a good trick on Perry. Ron had taken Paige into the bathroom and locked the door. Perry was outside the door. Ron shouted to Perry, "Tell your baby sister good-bye! I'm going to flush her down the toilet!" Ron laid Paige in the bathtub behind the door. Then he flushed the toilet. Next he came out of the bathroom without Paige and told Perry she was gone. Perry started to cry and scream. He ran into the bathroom and looked in the toilet. Finally, he found her in the bathtub. Until then, he really believed she was gone. Ron thought this was the biggest joke yet.

I began to doubt I could help Ron with his problems and still keep my children safe. How could his personality change so drastically from one moment to the next? I began to suspect he had more than one personality. Each month that went by the incidents were becoming more serious.

Soon Perry and Paige were old enough to have little friends over to play. Ron disliked all the neighbors. He never had contact with them so he had no reason for disliking them. He always said they were stupid bastards. Therefore, he disliked the neighbor children as well. He resented all my friends.

I began to take tranquilizers. Perry kept having severe stomach problems and Paige habitually wet the bed. Ron's problems were getting out of control.

In 1973, the most disturbing incident occurred. I was gone for about an hour and Ron was home with Perry (nine) and Paige (six). When I returned, Paige met me at the door. She seemed nearly hysterical. She said, "Mommy, mommy, do you know what daddy did to us? He took Perry and me down into the basement, and he threw lighted matches at us!" Ron thought it was a big joke. I felt sick. Inside I begged, "No more, no more, my God, no more!"

I knew a divorce would have to come, but felt afraid to go ahead with it. Talk of murder seemed to excite Ron. One evening Perry talked about what he wanted to be when he grew up. Ron interrupted and said, "When I grow up, I want to be a murderer." Almost daily he would talk about beating up other people. I just did not know how to handle him. I discussed the situation with two priests. They both said that in some cases, for the sake of the children, a divorce is acceptable.

I wanted to begin the divorce procedure right away but decided I must wait. Ron's father was terminally ill with cancer, and I knew a divorce at this time would be more than Ron could tolerate. We would have to find a way to survive until Ron's father passed away. After that Ron would need some time to heal. We waited some more.

The next few months were terrible. Ron's personalities were becoming more unstable. Some of the personalities were quite distinct, and I estimated there were at least five. As he changed from one personality to the other, I could detect slight changes in his voice. Sometimes I saw major differences in his face. One personality, a quiet soft-spoken adult, was the personality I fell in love with. It was also the personality that truly loved his children. Another personality seemed hostile and fascinated with violence and murder. This personality produced a dramatic change in his voice and face. (Sometimes I still have nightmares and can see that face.) Another of the personalities was that of a helpless child. During these times he seemed to lose the skills I knew he really had. There were other personalities I could detect but not identify. Some of the personalities were not aware of each other. Many times Ron did not have any recollection of events and behavior that he could not have forgotten. Clearly, there was poor communication between the personalities.

The threats came more frequent now. I begged Ron to some counseling but by the second session he quit! I went back for the third. The counselor felt that Ron definitely had a split personality. He said there is no certain cure for this condition and treatment can last for years. We could not last that long.

I needed to admit I could not fix Ron's problems. No matter how much I wanted to erase the emotional trauma that Ron suffered as a child, I could not do it.

Getting through the divorce process was frightening for the children and me. Ron threatened me constantly. Thanks be to God for restraining orders.

The divorce provided tremendous relief for the children and me. Paige's bed-wetting stopped immediately. Perry's stomach greatly improved. I threw away the tranquilizers. We felt ready for a fresh start. I went back to my old career as a bookkeeper and found a job that would allow me to be off work when Perry and Paige got home from school.

There were still some complications with visitation. Sometimes the children were afraid to go with Ron. We could never be sure which personality would surface during the visits. However, he found a girlfriend right away and that seemed to help a good deal. It took his focus off me. Therefore, he did not use the children to manipulate me and I was no longer his target.

Not long after that we heard Ron killed a man accidentally with his truck. It did not seem to thrill him as much as he had talked about months earlier. Shortly thereafter, he seemed even less thrilled when his latest girlfriend tried to do him in when he refused to marry her. Eventually he lost his truck driving job. That seemed sad. Ron was an extremely hard-working person and one of the best truck drivers around.

*Chapter 4*

# BEGINNING AGAIN

I wanted to re-establish friendships I had lost track of during the last years. I also wanted to learn to dance. Recruiting my brother Bud, the dancer of the family, it became his job to teach me. One night he came over and we rolled back the rugs in the basement and had a lesson. He proved to be a good teacher. A few months later there was a wedding in the family, and I was ready for the dance floor.

I met many of new people that night. One of them was a guy named Mike. He bought me a can of pop and asked me to dance. While we danced Mike asked me a few questions. He said that he was twenty-two and then asked, "How old are you?" I said, "I'm a little older than you." He said "How much older?" I said, "Take a guess." He replied, "Two or three years older?" I did not answer. I held up my ten fingers and he said, "I don't care, you sure look good to me." A few steps later I told Mike I was divorced with two small children. I expected him to trip over that statement, but he never missed a step. After more dancing and a few more cans of pop I told Mike good-bye and went home.

Several nights later a strange car drove into the yard. Mike had been fishing and he brought me the fish he had caught. I was not too keen on cleaning them so he did it for me. After that we spent a lot of time together going to dances, movies, and all kinds of social activities I missed in the past. He helped me with chores around the yard and I helped him with chores around his house.

Mike was Catholic. That was important to me. I was ten years older than Mike. That seemed unimportant to him. I was curious to see the children's reaction to Mike and his reaction to them.

A few months went by and surprisingly things went pretty well. Mike seemed to enjoy the children and they really liked the attention he gave them. We were all having a lot of fun.

A few more months went by and we decided to get married. Now there was a problem. I was divorced. If we got married, we would both be banned from the sacraments and most of the ceremonies of the church. This was a big deal!

I heard rumors of a new annulment program in the Catholic Church. I decided to visit our new priest and find out if it was true. Father T, recently ordained appeared friendly and interested in my situation. Everyone seemed to enjoy him. He told me annulments were possible, but the procedure was so new that he would need to make some inquiries and get back to me.

Within a few weeks Father T. called and asked me to come in. He had all the information and we went over the procedure. I soon learned it would be a long complicated process, possibly lasting a year or longer with no guarantees. Father T asked me if I felt sure I wanted to do this and I replied that I did. He told me that he would have little involvement with the procedure since each case is handed over to tribunal. He gave me some forms to fill out, which I promptly did.

Next, I needed to write my autobiography which proved to be quite a challenge. I really disliked writing and I would have to remember in detail the things about my marriage that I desperately wanted to forget. Gathering all my strength I began with my earliest childhood memories. I wrote mostly at night when everyone was asleep. After one full week of pain and misery I completed the autobiography. I felt exhausted and lost five pounds. This was not a good thing since I was already too thin.

Next came the interview with a member of the tribunal. I had no idea what to expect. It evolved into a grueling interrogation lasting five hours. It was a good thing I was truthful because this priest could spot a lie immediately. He would ask a question and a few hours later he would reword the question and ask it again. He seemed extremely skillful. At the end of the session my brain felt squeezed dry and I barely knew my own name. But he seemed satisfied.

With the autobiography and interview completed, Mike and I realized the next step would be months away. We decided to get married and continue the annulment procedure with the hope it would be granted someday. We found a Justice of the Peace and had a legal ceremony that felt more like buying a fishing license.

Mike always wanted a blonde, blue-eyed son to carry on his family's name. Mike was the last possibility to do that. Mike's father was an only child and Mike was his father's only son. When I became pregnant, I told Mike we might have a son but you married the wrong gal to get a blonde, blue-eyed boy. And then there was considerable controversy over whether it would be a boy or a girl. Mike and Perry (age eleven) ordered a boy. Paige (age eight) would respond, "Well, I ordered a girl. When you put your order in the mailbox, I went out there and ripped it up and replaced it with my order. So it is going to be a girl! Ha! Ha!" Around and around they went. I did not care if it was a boy or a girl as long as it was healthy and not too big.

By December 30, 1975 my body became enormous again. Our baby was due in two weeks. We planned a nice quiet New Year's holiday. That evening I decided to take down the Christmas tree, which exhausted me so I went to bed early. The following morning I discovered just how excited Mike could get.

When I awoke the bed felt wet and someone was on the way. At first Mike did not believe me because of my past history of going overdue. This was two weeks early! I suspected something might be wrong but did not say anything to the others. We grabbed some towels and headed for the hospital.

When we arrived at the hospital my doctor said, "Well, it looks like you're going to have a large tax deduction or a New Year's baby. Let's see what's going on." After some blood tests and x-rays, it became obvious that something was wrong! It was a condition called "placenta previa." That is: the placenta covers the cervical opening. During the delivery the baby's head pushes on the placenta; and when it ruptures, the baby and mother can bleed to death. My doctor advised us to have a Cesarean section to prevent the bleeding problem. We readily agreed.

A few hours later, Mark arrived. Mike and Perry got their boy. However, he was no blondie! Mark had a full head of nice brown hair and brown eyes. Paige's order for a little girl would have to wait until someday when she would have her own.

Mark was a large "preemie," well over nine pounds. When they put him in the incubator his head touched one end and his feet touched the other end. He looked extremely healthy, but it seemed obvious something was not right. He cried much more than the other babies. When we brought him home, the crying continued. He appeared to have severe colic. This was not too surprising since Mike had severe colic as an infant.

Paige had some colic as an infant, so we tried all the old remedies first. When that did not work, we tried all the new remedies. They did not work either. Soon Mark developed many respiratory infections and we all took turns in the rocking chair with him. We wore out one rocking chair and bought another. With all this attention going to Mark, I felt concerned that Perry and Paige would resent their new little brother. Sometimes I think they did, however, cuddling Mark seemed to come naturally to them.

When Mark was baptized, our annulment was not complete. During the Mass, Mike and I could not go to communion. We had to face the fact we might never be Catholic again. When we thought about that we came up with three options.

1. We could forget about going to church altogether. Many people do that.
2. We could choose another denomination that allows divorce and remarriage.
3. We could continue attending the Catholic Church and just not take part in the sacraments.

We decided the third option was best for us. We would not allow the Catholic Church to judge us. God would do that when we leave this world. We would continue to go to church in obedience to the third commandment and try to live a good life. We felt this option would be the most acceptable to God. Not going to Mass would be the least.

I had not heard anything about my annulment for months so I decided to inquire about its progress. I felt discouraged when I learned it was stalled indefinitely. An annulment requires interviews from both sides of the families. The interviews from my family were complete. However, there were no interviews from Ron or his family.

I decided to contact some of Ron's brothers and sisters with whom I had a good relationship in the past. Out of loyalty to Ron they refused to be interviewed. A few weeks later, Ron had to make a court appearance and I managed to talk to him for a few minutes. I knew he had stopped going to church. I figured he had nothing to lose by being interviewed. When I explained to him my future in the Catholic Church was at risk, he agreed to have an interview for a large sum of money.

There were three problems connected with his offer. First, we did not have that much money. Second, the interrogator was too clever. He would uncover the bribe. Third, I would not know which of Ron's personalities would do the talking.

*Now I Know Why*

Darn, this just did not seem fair. We had struggled and come such a long way and now we hit a brick wall. There had to be someone who could help us. I decided to try one more person. It would be a long shot, but at this point I had nothing to lose. Ron had a relative, Julie, whom I had met at various family events. She appeareded to be a particularly warm person and seemed interested in my children and me. Julie was a nurse and I could tell she was very good at what she did. She lived in the same city as Ron all the years he was growing up. She had first hand knowledge of his family background, information the tribunal required. The problem was, Julie had nothing to gain by helping me. On the contrary, she would be taking quite a risk. She seemed to be my last hope.

I gathered all my courage and called Julie to ask if I could see her alone. She told me she would arrange her schedule so I could. One morning after her family left the house; I went over to see her. I explained the situation. She seemed concerned about Ron's threats to us and his unstable behavior. I explained to her the tribunal wanted a two-hour interview in person. However, under the circumstances, they would consider doing the interview over the phone. It would have to be recorded. I could see she felt reluctant. We talked awhile longer, and it must have seemed to her that I was begging. I guess maybe I was.

Finally, she agreed with one stipulation. She said, "You must promise never tell anyone I did this. You see, I'm frightened, too." I agreed.

A few weeks later the interview was completed. The annulment was granted. It was the second annulment granted in our diocese. I felt so grateful to Julie and sad that I could not do something to show it. On the

*Audre Kramer*

contrary, I had to sever all ties with her to ensure her safety. I knew that Julie would occupy a special place in my heart.

On February 21, 1976, Mike and I had our marriage blessed at a short ceremony during Mass. Once again, our family of five shared the same religion.

*Chapter 5*

# TROUBLE WITH THE P_____ WORD

One summer day in 1977, I went to visit my older brother, Bud, at his automobile shop. I do not remember the exact reason, although it must have been for some minor repair since I brought Mark (one and a half years old) with me. "Before you leave," Bud asked, "would you like to see my new motorcycle?" I have always liked shiny things with wheels and told him I would love to see it.

He explained that he and Les had bought bikes and planned to take a trip out west and probably join a cycle club. As we approached the motorcycle, I identified it as a Honda Gold Wings. It looked beautiful! He seemed so proud to show it to me. Almost instantly a feeling of dread consumed me. It is difficult to explain how this felt, except that I knew something terrible would happen involving the bike! As he explained some of the features, I could hardly stand to look at it and immediately switched my gaze to the floor. Dread turned to fear, and I desperately wanted to leave.

With a big grin Bud said, "It's so nice out, let's start it up and go for a short ride." I replied, "We can't take Mark with us and I won't leave him alone." Bud persisted and said, "You can put Mark in the car for a few minutes and pull the keys. He will be fine because we're out here in the country and the landscape is flat. We will be able to see him if we stay close by." He was almost pleading with me to go, and I felt terrible when I refused. How could I explain that the sight of the bike made me feel sick? He must have thought I was jealous or something. I did not have a real excuse to give him. I could not wait to leave, but it saddened me to have him feel I did not want to share his joy about something so important to him.

As I drove home, I tried to understand what happened. Nothing like this ever happened before, and it did not make any sense. I decided my reaction must be foolishness. I could make it up to him somehow, and I let it go at that.

A few weeks later I went to visit my other brother, Les, and his family. They were a hard working couple who also knew how to have a good time. Typically they were bubbly and easygoing. They owned a large crop farm, and Les worked in the fields, while I visited with his wife, Barb. We walked around the yard as the kids played. Barb said, "Hey would you like to see our bike? We're going to take a trip out west with Bud and his wife. It's really going to be fun, and Les is looking forward to getting away for a while. It's in the garage, let's take a look!" Before I could think about it, we were standing in front of the bike. Sure enough, it was another Honda Gold Wings beauty. It even had a trailer to match. Barb seemed so excited she did not seem to notice my response.

*Now I Know Why*

That same terrible feeling hit me again, but this time it seemed much worse. I felt like I was suffocating. I quickly began to study the clutter on the floor. I pretended to be happy because I could not see what else to do. I just wanted to get away and breathe some fresh air. I do not know how long we were in the garage, but it seemed like forever.

As we left the garage, their daughter, Shawn (eleven years old), whizzed past us on her dirt bike and headed down their long driveway. She was a little speedster, and Barb shouted after her, "Shawn if you get hurt on that thing, you're going to get it." She giggled in her usual easygoing manner, and inside I wanted to scream. I cannot remember how I excused myself and left, but somehow I did. I felt numb.

For a time I would not let myself think about the events of those days. There was nothing to do but deny what I felt when I looked at the "Gold Wings" insignia. What could I say? Who would understand? What did it mean? I told myself it was ridiculous. I tried not to think about it, yet I knew they would be taking their trip west very soon. Fear about the different roads, long hours of driving, possible bad weather and steep mountains tortured me. I felt sure if there were going to be an accident, it would be on that trip.

I did not even want to know the date of the trip. I could not stand to think of it. I wanted to block it out. I had some success doing that because of my hectic schedule with my family.

In mid August I learned they all returned safe and sound. They had a great trip. Elvis Presley died while they were gone. Years later, during a conversation with Bud I realized both events occurred at the same time.

It seemed such a relief to have them back home. Fall came quickly and the motorcycles were stored away for winter. I felt sure now that the terrible premonition, or whatever it was, should be forgotten and let my busy schedule wipe away the memory.

By now it seemed obvious that Mark (age eighteen months) had some serious health problems. He felt sick every day with chronic respiratory infections or chronic stomach problems. Many times medication only made him sicker. The local general practitioners were baffled. Mark appeared healthy. That is, he was not underweight and he always seemed to have too much energy. Yet he was always sick, sometimes critically, and he cried endlessly. It became a full time job to keep him alive and relatively healthy. Sometimes I felt the doctors did not believe what I was telling them. Finally I demanded they refer Mark to the University of Minnesota. I think they agreed just to get us out of their office.

Four specialists at the university examined Mark. They were dumbfounded at the list of food that he could not tolerate. They decided he had an enzyme deficiency (chemical in the stomach needed to digest food) and some food allergies. They did many tests and told us they would send the results to us in a month.

During that time I went to visit my cousin, Lois. (Years earlier, she accompanied me when I rode that bicycle down a steep hill and wiped out.) As we visited I explained Mark's problems to her. She replied, "Gosh, that sounds like my kids. They are allergic to cow's milk so we switched them to goat's milk, and they improved rapidly. I'll send a gallon home with you to get you started." I felt skeptical but was willing to try anything.

That afternoon I gave Mark his first bottle of goat's milk, then another bottle that evening. We went to bed and expected the usual routine of taking turns every few hours to rock Mark during the night. The next morning when I awoke, I realized Mark had not cried all night. I thought he must have died because he had never slept one whole night since he was born. I felt frightened as I walked into the nursery. As I got closer to the crib, I could tell he was still breathing. Then it was obvious. Mark was sound asleep. He had actually slept all night! I could not believe it.

Within a week Mark's chronic diarrhea, cramps and diaper rash were gone. Within six weeks his respiratory infections were clearing up. About that time his test results from the University finally arrived. They confirmed Mark's allergy to cow's milk and several other foods. In addition there was a long list of foods he was not allergic to, but still could not eat because of his enzyme problem. By giving Mark all the goat's milk he wanted and other safe foods, he started to live a normal life. He could play and learn and do the things other kids do without being sick. With that, all of our lives improved.

Spring 1978 found us busy collecting buildings for a small dairy goatherd. We were tired of driving fifty miles to buy goat's milk, and the people running the dairy were ready to retire. We found a small barn seven miles away that could be moved to our farm. My brother Les agreed to take the job; and what a job it was!

Les was a master at figuring out most anything. He jacked up the barn (16' x 24') and rolled two telephone poles under it, to act as runners. He attached a log chain to the ends of the poles and hitched the chain to his huge Versatile tractor. We literally pulled the barn down the road.

Two miles from home we wore out the poles and dropped the whole thing in the middle of the road. What to do? Well, Les just took a chain saw and went into a nearby woods. He cut two poplar trees and trimmed off the branches. "Presto," he had two new poles. Needless to say, this attracted quite a bit of attention. During this process someone must have called the sheriff. When he arrived, he did not seem happy. After a heated discussion he said, "Get this thing out of here", and we did. The last two miles went off without a hitch.

May seemed a busy month with long work days. We finished remodeling our barn and Les planted his crops. One evening after a particularly busy day, Mike and I joined our neighbors for a trip to the Dairy Queen. It was a nice warm spring evening, and we enjoyed a

*Now I Know Why*

chance to visit. As we ate our sundaes the fire whistle blew. A few minutes later we could hear several sirens and when the trucks did not go in our direction we commented, "Glad it's not for us, the kids are home alone." We finished our treats and started home. We speculated the flurry of activity probably had something to do with the prom night activities.

We arrived home fifteen minutes later, and I began to get the kids ready for bed. The phone rang. I answered. My brother, Bud, was on the other end. His voice sounded strained but steady. He said, "I am at the hospital. There has been an accident. We were on our way home from Hutchinson with the cycle club when a car struck Les and Barb's cycle. They are hurt pretty bad. They have broken arms and legs, but both are conscious. One of Les's legs is really bad. Can you get Mom and Dad, and bring them here?" I replied, "We'll be right there!"

My heart sank. I remembered the premonition. We hurried to collect Mom and Dad, but all the while my thoughts were racing from, "This can't be happening, this can't be happening," to "Please God, please let them be all right. Broken bones aren't so bad. Please, God, please let them be all right." I attempted to distract myself from the premonition and tried to keep my mother calm. A few years earlier she suffered a serious heart attack and this would be difficult at best.

When we arrived at the hospital, the nurses were closing the doors to the emergency room. Les lay inside. As I attempted to learn about his condition, Bud's wife took me aside. She and Bud had been riding right behind Les and Barb.

She stated, "Barb has been taken upstairs. Both her legs and one arm are broken. She is pressing the doctors to set them now, but they need to evaluate her condition first. Will you go up and explain to her that it's best to wait? You know about things like that, maybe she will listen to you." I agreed. I left the emergency area and ran up to her room. Her condition appeared to be grave. She was held together with splints. One foot was attached by skin only. Considering her injuries, she seemed very alert. We talked a few minutes and I convinced her to follow the doctor's advice.

I hurried back down to the emergency room. The doors were still closed, but there was steady traffic in and out. I could not get any information other than Les's leg was laying over his shoulder when he landed in the ditch, and he was conscious when he came in. The nurses moved our family to the lobby. As I comforted Mother, Mike pulled me aside. He said, "I just caught one of the nurses coming out of the emergency room. She told me they don't think Les is going to make it!" I doubted him. I questioned him, "Are you sure?" He replied, "That's what she said; do you think you should call someone?" I could not let myself believe any of this. Reluctantly, I located a phone and called a priest. Then, I completed a call to my sister. As I hung up the telephone I glanced down the hall. I saw Bud walking away from the emergency room; his friend had his arm around him. Inside I screamed, "NO! NO! NO! This can't be happening!"

*Now I Know Why*

Les was dead!

After the funeral I reflected on some of the events. I did not have the words to describe this incident. As I searched the dictionary I found the word, "premonition: a notification or warning of what is to come; forewarning." I did not like this word because I always associated it with phony-baloney entertainers on television. Now I am forced to use this word until they make a better one.

The suffocating feeling I experienced when I looked at Les's bike several months earlier, matched the last hour of his life. With an oxygen mask on his face, he repeatedly pulled it off, and said, "I can't breathe, I can't breathe." This is the sensation one can feel while bleeding to death.

The night of the accident Les and Barb were riding on their cycle, ahead of Bud and his wife. Usually they rode side by side, but that night they were riding single file. Bud escaped the accident. Yet the premonition (gee, I hate that word) involved both brothers. Was Bud spared that night when they decided to ride single file instead of side by side?  Or was the dread I sensed, the emotional trauma Bud incurred while trying to comfort his dying brother in the ditch?

When the accident occurred Les's bike started to burn.  The first call requested an ambulances and a fire truck.  Early bystanders and the members from the cycle club put the fire out.  When they called to cancel the fire truck, the ambulances were also canceled.  When the ambulances failed to arrive, another call was placed.  They were dispatched again.  It took one hour to reach the hospital nine miles away.  Officially Les died from traumatic injuries that caused him to bleed to death.  Those lost minutes might have made a difference.  Maybe not.

Also, there was considerable doubt about the doctor's condition that night.  He had quite a reputation for drinking.  We were very dissatisfied with his performance.  In the emergency room, this doctor spent his time sewing up Les's shattered leg.  All the while Les was bleeding to death internally.  Years later this doctor would play another important role in my life.

Afterwards I thought about what happened.  Premonitions are impossible.  After all, I had never heard or read about anything like this in my science or medical books.  It just could not be.  No, could not happen, does not happen.  No!  No!  No!  It had to be a cruel coincidence, a joke, plain nonsense and ridiculous, any one of the above.  I vowed to bury this memory with Les.  Although in the years that followed, I would awaken at night, and the memory would return.  In the safety of the darkness, tears crept onto my pillow.

After Les's death I could see a change in my Dad. He started to be more concerned about his remaining children. Sometimes he fixed broken tools, etc. for us, or helped with other tasks. He seemed to be developing into a pretty fair grandfather, too. He seemed to enjoy taking the grandchildren hunting and fishing. He spent many hours telling them stories about his adventures, and his tales fascinated them.

*Chapter 6*

# BEING JERKED AROUND

January, 1986, I made an appointment for my annual checkup with my gynecologist in St. Cloud, Minnesota. Usually booked far in advance, I called a few months early and made the appointment for the beginning of March, 1986.

On February 17, 1986, (three weeks before my appointment) I was doing my routine floor exercises while watching television. As I rolled onto my stomach I felt something unusual. It did not actually hurt and I assumed it was probably gas. I mentioned something about it to my husband, Mike, and he replied, "My stomach does not feel too good either. I think I am coming down with the flu." I expected the next morning we would both be sick.

The next morning arrived and we both felt fine. I headed off to work. I assisted elderly and handicapped people in their homes and went to my first client, a lady in her late 70's. She wore a heavy brace on her leg and was nearly deaf. She seemed a cheerful person and I always looked forward to seeing her. While caring for her needs, I suddenly stopped my work and went to the phone to call the local clinic. I heard myself asking for an appointment that afternoon and asked who would be available. The receptionist replied, "All the doctors are booked except for one." The doctor who was available was the same doctor who cared for Les in the emergency room the night of his accident and death. Recalling the dissatisfaction we felt, I remembered saying to myself, I would not see him for a cold or a pimple. At the same time a voice came out of me saying, "I'll take the appointment."

I would like to make an analogy at this point about this incident. It was like getting into a car and driving to Minneapolis. When you get there and get out of the car, you find you are in St. Cloud. When I left my home on the morning of February 18, to go to work; I actually went to the doctor without being aware of that decision. I was literally being jerked around, and it felt like someone else controlled me.

When I entered the doctor's office, he asked what he could do for me. I replied I did not really know why I was there but felt something might wrong. This is really out of character for me. Usually when I see a doctor, I state my problem precisely and discuss the expected treatment in detail. He seemed a little confused by my reply and started to ask a few questions. Are you sick, having any pain, running a temperature, having abnormal periods, etc? I answered no to everything but then told him of the twinge I felt in my stomach the night before. He seemed perplexed and replied, "Well, since you're here, I might as well examine you." He adjusted the table and I reclined. As he felt my abdominal area, his face grew solemn. He said, "I definitely feel something." He called the nurse and prepared me for a more thorough examination. The internal exam revealed a large mass in my abdomen. His said that it was probably a tumor in my uterus. I was not having problems and had yearly checkups. At age, forty-two, it was probably a fibroid tumor, since they can grow very fast and very large. He stated he could operate by the end of the week.

This was hardly what I expected to hear. I was in shock and it took me a few minutes to process this. As he prepared to schedule the surgery, I collected myself and stated I had a specialist in St. Cloud. Also I had an appointment for the first week in March and I definitely planned to see him. He replied, "You can't wait that long." Clearly irritated by my statement and he grumbled something about doing operations like this all the time. Abruptly he said, "Who is this doctor anyway? I'll have to call him and have your appointment moved up." I gave him the name and phone number and he left the room. Upon returning to my room his demeanor seemed more friendly. He said, "I talked to your gynecologist and your appointment has been moved up to February 20, two days from now. I wish you the best of luck." I thanked him and left the room.

Totally stunned, I drove home with a million thoughts going through my mind. Who would take care of Mark (age ten)? It was my responsibility to care for our large dairy goat herd. How could Mike do that and work, too? Who would take care of my clients while I recovered? I had not been laid up for a long time. How do I do this?

I got home before Mike and Mark and spent the time thinking about how to manage the next few weeks. After a while it did not seem too bad; we could do this. By the time they got home I had most things sorted out

*Now I Know Why*

and felt ready to explain the situation matter of factly. After all, I had not even seen my gynecologist, and he might have a different diagnosis.

The next two days passed quickly. Fairly confident I presented myself at the gynecologist's office on Thursday. However, his examination and opinion were nearly the same. He began, "Well, there was nothing there eleven months ago so whatever it is grew very fast. It is so large it must be a fibroid, but I can't tell for sure. It could be attached to your ovary. Whatever it is, it has to come out. Let me check my schedule." He left the room and when he returned he stated, "I have you scheduled for one week from tomorrow." I was really disappointed. Now that I knew for sure there was a tumor and I would have to have an operation, I wanted it over with. I frowned and said, "You mean I have to carry this thing around for a whole week?" He paused and said, "Let me check again." He left the room a second time and when he returned he stated, "You'll be first on Monday morning." That felt so much better.

I adjusted quickly to having this surgery. A fibroid tumor is not very serious. I could be out of the hospital in a few days and almost back to normal in a month. I decided there should not be anything else to worry about. I felt great. I never smoked or drank. There was not any cancer in my immediate family. This should be easy. I felt confident and the rest of my family did too.

I wanted to feel the tumor myself. Since it was large and I was slim, I should be able to locate it by pressing on my abdomen, ...not so easy. Then I laid on my back on the floor and felt all over, ...no luck. Then I breathed in, pulling my stomach in and there it was, ...big and hard like a

*Audre Kramer*

grapefruit. I let my husband and kids feel it. "Yep," they replied, "it's there all right."

There was just a weekend to make all the arrangements at home. It was difficult to tell my clients who depended on me that I could not care for them for at least a month. They were all concerned and wished me well.

On Monday morning, February 24, 1986, Mike and I entered the hospital. I felt upbeat and confident and Mike seemed fairly calm, considering his high strung nature.

After an uneventful admission, they sent me to a preoperative room. An anesthesiologist came in to see me. He asked about any problems with my three earlier surgeries. I informed him that with two of them I woke up too soon. With one I awoke quickly and hypos were not effective to control the postoperative pain. With the other, a more minor surgery, I woke up while still on the operating table. He replied, "Well, I'll see to it that it won't happen this time. You'll sleep at least a couple of hours afterward." That sounded good. And so it began.

My next recollection seemed like I was coming out of a terrible darkness. The pain seemed unbearable. At first I thought they were still cutting me and I awoke too soon. I cried out and a nurse came to my side. I begged her for a shot. She said she could not do anything because my doctor thought I would sleep several hours and he had already started his next surgery. Without his order she could do nothing. Trapped again! Oh God, this hurt, so bad! I ground my teeth like crazy.

I faded in and out of consciousness for what seemed like hours. Finally, I awoke with two doctors at my side. I asked them what I had. I

*Now I Know Why*

expected them to say it was just a fibroid tumor. One of them looked at me and said, "You have cancer. We removed a large tumor." I was in such pain it did not matter what they said. I begged for anything to relieve the pain. They ordered a hypo and started to move me to the postoperative ward. As they rolled me down a hall, the elevator doors came open and my oldest son, Perry, stepped out. We spoke for a second and they moved me on. He was supposed to be at the university. I could not understand why he was at the hospital. Later I learned when the doctor gave my husband the grim news, he quickly summoned my son. The immediate outlook seemed poor, at best. With the extensive surgery and I required transfusions to offset the bleeding. The cancer appeared to be advanced.

My husband, unprepared for this situation, needed someone to hold on to. "It is not supposed to be this way!" Fortunately, his parents and sisters were near by. He needed to run to them, yet he needed to stay. Somehow he did both. He had to inform our other children and my family. Never having experienced something like this, coupled with his high strung nature, proved to be quite a challenge. During the following surgeries, he never sat in the waiting room alone again.

The first twenty-four hours after surgery felt like hell on earth. The pain seemed relentless. They might as well have squirted the hypos on the floor. I so envied other people who could sleep those first days after surgery. The teeth grinding continued and my jaw became extremely painful.

By the second and third day I started to ask questions, and the answers were not encouraging. The doctors were solemn and to the point. The tumor was cancerous, large (small cantaloupe size) and attached to everything it touched. They must have had a garbage can next to the operating table to hold everything they took out. The list of what was removed was very long. They said I would need six months of chemotherapy, and then they would operate again to see what was left. Of course, I knew that if anything was left, it would also kill me.

My recovery seemed speedy considering the procedure. When I got home, I had a difficult time waiting for the test results from the Mayo Clinic. They would be more exact than the initial tests. In the meantime, I started to research ovarian cancer. I discovered it was called, "The Silent Killer." You never know it is there until it has spread. Since my tumor was attached to everything, it surely must have spread. At least that was the message my surgeons were sending. From what I could gather, I was most likely a Stage III candidate, which translated to a fifteen percent chance to live up to five years.

The waiting was terrible. The more I researched, the more I knew. The more I knew, the harder it was to wait. In the meantime I was assigned to an oncologist with an appointment to review my tests. Finally, I would learn my fate. I felt afraid to find out, but not knowing seemed much worse.

My oncologist, a dark-haired man was soft spoken and slim. As he discussed my case, he seemed surprised at the knowledge I had, and asked if I was a nurse or something. I replied, "Medicine and science were hobbies that had gotten out of hand." He realized that I wanted all the answers, and he complied.

He opened my file and began. He said, "The lab tests from the Mayo clinic are much different than we expected. Upon examining all the tissue samples, they were unable to find cancer cells outside the tumor. However, that does not mean they are not there. Cells could have been shed into your blood stream and traveled to other parts of your body. Removing the tumor was difficult because it was attached to your colon, bladder, uterus, literally everything it touched. Also, the outer membrane of the tumor was very thin, and cells could have been lost while removing it. Mayo has classed you at Stage I, but I am advising you to undergo chemotherapy for six months. We will do a second look surgery after that." He went into detail about the harsh treatment ahead. My first chemotherapy would be four weeks after the surgery. That would allow enough time for my incision to heal so it could withstand the severe vomiting that would occur.

I listened carefully to the doctor's words. I focused on the possibility of being stage 1 instead of stage III. When he finished explaining the procedures, he asked if I had any questions. I was waiting with a big one and said, "Doctor, if I'm stage I, why do I have to undergo all that misery?" He replied, "Because the lab technician couldn't see what the surgeons saw." He implied that the test results could be flawed. It was almost as if the lab tests did not match the surgeon's report. It became clear to me then that all my doctors had some strong reservations about my prognosis. It did not matter to me whether the test results were faulty or not, I needed to believe I had a chance to survive

Before my first chemotherapy treatment, I had to return to my gynecologist for a final check up. He agreed with the oncologist that chemotherapy was necessary. That settled it. But before I left I needed to ask one more question, which had troubled me from the beginning. I said,

*Audre Kramer*

"What if something hadn't forced me to that first doctor on February 18, 1986? What if I had waited a few weeks until the appointment I made for my yearly check-up? What would have happened?"

He paused for a moment, then softly replied, "You didn't have another couple of weeks, probably not a couple of days. The membrane around the tumor was extremely thin; I can't believe I got it out without breaking it. If it had broken before we operated the cells would have quickly spread throughout your body. There were two types of cancer in the tumor that formed a deadly combination for which there is no effective treatment."

*Chapter 7*

# CHEMO-A TRIP TO HELL

Four weeks passed since the surgery and I regained some strength and a few pounds. I purchased a wig in advance so that I would have it on the day my hair would fall out. I felt as ready as I could get.

March 27, 1986, arrived. Mike and I walked toward the clinic. He stopped a moment and said, "I wish I could do this for you." I replied, "I know you do, but you can't. Other people go through this and I can too."

The nurses prepped me for my treatment and asked me a multitude of questions. They weighed me, measured me, and checked my fat content. All seemed to be part of an equation to determine how much Cisplatin and Cytoxan my body could tolerate. When all was ready, they led me to a small room, much like a closet. In it was an IV pole and a large vinyl brown recliner. (I still cringe whenever I see one.) They put a large needle in my arm that could handle a heavy flow. The treatment consisted of nearly a gallon of solution. It took four hours to deliver all of it. I will never forget the taste in my mouth, something like sucking on a dirty nickel. Part way through, my intestinal tract started to empty. I had difficulty understanding simple directions. I felt extremely sick and I asked if I could stay in the hospital just overnight. They said the insurance company would not allow it. That did not make sense, but I did not want them to think I was a baby, either. Reluctantly we began the thirty-five mile trip home. I felt terribly uncomfortable and vomited every ten minutes. Good thing we brought a bucket.

When we got home, I went straight to bed. Following my doctor's instructions I armed myself with a glass of liquid, a teaspoon and a bucket. He said, "No matter how much you vomit, you must drink a little, even if it's just a spoonful."

The next few hours were torture. I lay in my bed trying to drink; then trying to get my head over the bucket. My friend, Marge, came into the bedroom to check on me. She asked if there was anything she could do to help me. I replied, "No." Mike had just brought me more water and emptied my bucket. I sat on the edge of the bed for a few minutes and wiped my face. Marge sat next to me. After a few minutes she said, "I have to move away from you. Your body is so hot that you are making me feel too warm." A few minutes later she left and I reclined again.

The next twenty hours consisted of non-stop vomiting. There seemed no chance for fluid intake. Getting my head over the bucket proved a major problem. My body continued to get hotter, and the vomit seemed to boil out of me. They said I would be sick. Is this what they meant? They never said I would get so hot. Because my judgment was terribly impaired I complied with the insurance company's order not to return to the hospital. Sensing that death was nearby I scribbled some notes on a scrap of paper so that the doctors would know what went wrong. I prayed, "God help me, I am getting cooked."

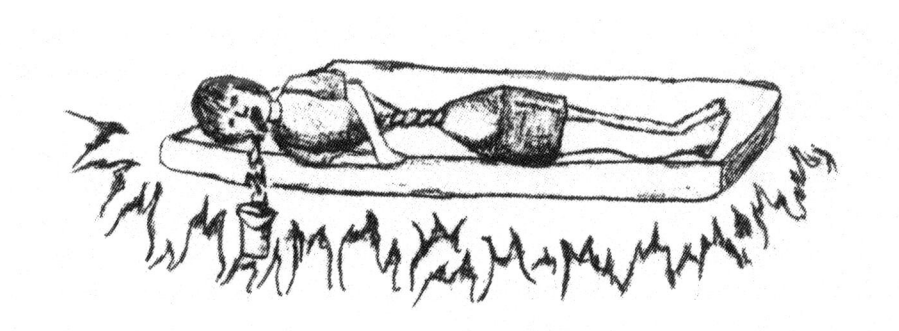

The second day seemed a little better. I managed one tablespoon of liquid per hour. The third and fourth day I finally ate small amounts of food. My stomach remained unsettled for ten more days. In spite of all the wrenching my incision remained intact but very painful.

Quickly my attention shifted to the next dilemma. My eyes became extremely light sensitive. It felt like my eyes were being fried. Headaches occurred every day. I slept in a room with the heavy shades and had to wear sunglasses to come out. To go outside I needed to wear dark desert sunglasses, plus a hat pulled over my eyebrows. Even then my eyes still throbbed.

When I returned to my oncologist, he seemed surprised at the severity of my reaction to the chemotherapy. At first he said I would be hospitalized for the next treatment, even though the insurance company would object. However, he left the room for a few minutes, and when he returned he said it was too risky to have another treatment like the first one. The next treatment would be reduced to Cytoxan only. Cisplatin was the culprit here, but it was also the most effective drug.

The second treatment seemed better, not much different than a bad flu. However, my eyes were getting worse and the oncologist felt we should stop chemotherapy all together. It seemed too risky to go on, and Cytoxan by itself is usually not effective with this type of cancer. I would just have to hope for the best.

It became clear that I needed an ophthalmologist to assess my eye problems. The doctor had never seen a case exactly like mine and could not tell me what to expect. My eyes could continue to get worse until I would be blind, they might just stay like they were, or they might return to normal. I would have to wait and see. If the cancer returned, it would not be a big deal anyway.

By this time, I had lost about half of my long hair. When I cut it shorter it looked fairly good and I returned the wig. Funny how good that felt, at least something went right.

The next couple of months spring turned into early summer. I used that time to gain some strength. I tried to focus on one day at a time and forget about the past and what might lie ahead. By the end of July, things took a turn for the worse. Something went terribly wrong in my stomach, and I ended up in the hospital with an obstructed bowel. In the emergency room the doctor opted to run a nasogastric tube through my nose and down my throat and into my stomach. Darn, that was a miserable procedure. I wished they had put me to sleep. I told myself, "Once like that should be enough in a lifetime." There were hours of teeth grinding before they got me stabilized.

We hoped the tube would allow my stomach to rest while they used IV's to keep me going. In five or six days I felt much better and they released me from the hospital. Discharge orders included a baby food diet and further tests to determine the cause of the problem. Of course, I knew the timing was perfect for another tumor to have formed. Most likely cancer was the real problem. Before all the tests were completed, my bowel became obstructed again. The need for surgery was apparent, but now I seemed a poor candidate. There hadn't been enough time to recover from all the trauma of the past six months. How could I face the terrible postoperative pain again and worse yet, the long drawn out misery of dying of cancer? If the cancer had returned, I secretly wished the doctor would not wake me up after surgery. Of course, I knew that was not an option.

The day of the surgery an anesthesiologist came to see me with good news. He said, "I see by your chart, you have problems with postoperative pain. We have something new to try on patients like you. It is called an epidural infusion and early tests are very encouraging. We insert a small tube near your spine and pump medicine through it. With a little luck, you will be pain free for several days." Yeah, right! I had heard too many promises before to fall for that line. But what the heck; it could not be any worse, so why not try it?

Well, well, well, what a change of luck! Not only did the epidural work, but the bowel obstruction was not caused by recurring cancer! It was an adhesion (scar tissue) instead! I could not believe it. The surgeon seemed surprised too. He told Mike, "You know when we opened her up, I was afraid to look in there. We looked everything over, and right now there's no sign of cancer." That was great news. However there was bad news too! A second look surgery should be twelve months after the onset, not six months. Six months is not long enough to give a reliable prognosis. I would have to undergo another surgery in a few months or a year. Oh well, at least things looked all right for now.

I really needed some time to recover. All this trauma took a terrible toll. I lost a lot of weight, felt terribly weak and my eyes were no better, but no worse either.

*Chapter 8*

# A LITTLE BIT OF LIGHT

I learned some things about myself during the six months of surgeries, chemotherapy and recuperation. I always liked being outdoors. After all the time in the hospital and lying home in bed, I started to dislike being indoors. I felt almost claustrophobic. I snuck outside for any reason and if too sick to go out, I consoled myself by sitting in our precious bay window. I invested in a large pile of sunglasses and various hats. The sun still felt painful since my eyes had not improved

Two weeks after my release from the hospital, I felt overjoyed to return. This time it was for a special event. My son and his wife were about to become parents. I went to the waiting room and after a few minutes my son came in. He stated things were moving very slowly and Peggy seemed to be having a hard time. No one else was there, so I asked Perry if I could see Peggy for a few minutes. He returned to her room to ask if it would be all right. She said it would be fine.

I went to her room planning to be there for a few minutes. A few minutes turned into many hours. The labor turned out to be long and difficult. All three of us worked as a team. Perry rubbed Peggy's back during the contractions. I held her hand and was the timekeeper. Peggy did all the work. It proved to be a long hard day and finally Mollie Teresa was born. Now a bright star shone amidst all the gloom and doom that surrounded me.

Around this time I learned that Eileen, another member of our little country church, was also diagnosed with ovarian cancer. She lived three miles away. She was a little older than I and very ill. I felt surprised there was another case so close. A few months later, February 1987, Eileen died. Clearly this disease deserved its reputation as a killer.

My oncologist scheduled checkups every three months, and I made sure I never missed an appointment. My March 1987, appointment turned out to be very disturbing. My mammogram came back with unidentified tissue that had not there before. My doctor ordered a magnified mammogram and other tests to make a diagnosis. Breast cancer would fit right into this scenario. I knew the odds were against me and the long wait to get all the test results seemed unbearable. Would this be the time when my luck runs out? Death always seemed to lurk just a few steps behind me. Finally the results arrived. Good luck again! They determined the spots were calcified tissue, not great, but not cancer. For now we could safely observe it for other changes.

In May of 1987, Alice, another member of our small church, died of cancer. Someone said they thought it was ovarian cancer. I did not want to know. Later I learned that it was ovarian and that it was discovered at the earliest stage, much earlier than mine. They found it by accident while addressing an unrelated problem. She had been told it was completely removed and it should not recur. She lived three and a half miles away. It frightened me to hear that Alice died of the same disease. I needed more time to get used to the idea that I would die, too.

By now my eyes stabilized and on cloudy days, I could get by with sunglasses and no hat. The headaches were nearly gone. I began to think that blindness would not be part of my life.

The next hurdle was that third look surgery. I had been putting it off but knew that was unwise. I just did not want to face another surgery. I actually started to feel pretty good. I had a full summer and now autumn arrived, my favorite time of the year. Still I desperately wanted to know if I was cancer free.

The surgery was set for October 29, 1987, twenty months after the onset. If they did not find anything, I could begin to be a little more optimistic. It seemed pretty basic. Cut out the old scar, go in and look around. Take out some lymph nodes for testing and use the epidural infusion for postoperative pain; simple enough. Well, not quite.

*Audre Kramer*

The epidural did its job for pain control but another problem developed. Every time I fell asleep, I stopped breathing. That set off an alarm and nurses came running to arouse me. It seemed eerie at first but when it kept happening, it became annoying. I really needed to sleep and after a while it felt more like torture. They opened my gown and watched my chest movement, hoping to relocate the sensors to a better spot. That did not help. After two days and twenty alarms, I could finally breathe and sleep at the same time.

Aside from this, the surgery went well. The results could not have been better, no cancer anywhere! I really felt relieved. Every month that went by without recurrence improved my odds. Now they were fifty/fifty. Even if it did come back, I should be able to last another year.

*Chapter 9*

# TROUBLE WITH THE T\_\_\_\_ WORD

I recovered quickly from this surgery and after a few months, decided to go back to work, just a few hours a week to start. We planned to buy a new van, and the extra money would come in handy. We could not decide what to do with our Ford Granada. It was eleven years old but still a good car. We talked about selling it or just keeping it. We ordered our van in June of 1988, and it was due to arrive that following August. We waited impatiently for it to arrive.

During this time another unexplainable incident occurred. It seemed similar to the premonition in 1977 when I knew something terrible would happen to Les. I did not see a vision and I did not hear a voice. The information completely by-passed my five senses. It was just there, without any action on my part.

The incident recurred several times when I thought about what to do with the Granada. At first the information was: "There is no reason to decide what to do with it. It is going to be in an accident, and there will be nothing to sell or keep." I dismissed the whole thing and decided to think about it another day.

Several days later I thought about the Granada again. This time the information became more distinct. "There will be an accident and you will be driving." However, there was no fear connected to the information. I felt I would not be killed, maybe not even injured. I began to feel uncomfortable. I thought. *This stuff just does not happen!* I needed to clear this out of my head and enjoy the thought of our new van arriving.

Finally a decision needed to be reached. I just wanted to get it over with. We will sell the Granada, and I would not have to think about it any more. When I accomplished that, the final information arrived. "There will be an accident. You will be driving. You will be struck by some type of law enforcement vehicle. You will say to Mike, "Well I guess we don't have to think about selling the Granada, the ( ? ) just bought it." Again, there was no feeling of fear. There was not a day or a time given. The screen went blank so-to-speak.

Well, that was enough of that. I thought, *This is ridiculous! Absolutely, nothing is going to happen. Nothing. Not a thing. Even if it does, I will survive. But nothing is going to happen—but—just in case—I will drive extra carefully, and I will refuse to accept any more information.* If I accepted this, I would have to accept all the earlier incidents, and I couldn't do that.

About a week later Mike, Perry and I went to my cousin, Donna's, anniversary dance. I was looking forward to seeing many of my relatives that I had not seen for years. Mike and I really enjoy dancing, and we were getting pretty good at it. We got all gussied up, put on our dancing shoes, and headed out for an evening of fun.

I had a nap that day so I drove home. It was after midnight and extremely dark. A storm was brewing behind us; I could see the lightning in my rearview mirror. The air felt heavy and my bright headlights cut through the thick darkness like a sharp knife. Mike and Perry slept as I drove home.

A mile and a half from home we came around a sharp hairpin curve. As I entered the curve I could hear wheels squealing, but could not see where it was coming from. There were no other lights anywhere. Out of the darkness, another car zoomed in front of me. As it ripped the front of my car away, I got a glimpse of a big star on the door. Then my headlights were gone and everything was dark. I remember the sound of breaking glass, smashing metal, sparks flying and my car swinging around. It seemed to last forever. Even with my seat belt on, my body jerked around like a rag doll.

When the car stopped moving it seemed apparent that Michael and Perry were not hurt; thank God. They scrambled out of our car. Perry stayed near me while Michael ran over to the other car. The driver was out of his car and leaning against it. He appeared to be in pain, but not seriously injured. Michael seemed surprised to discover it was a deputy sheriff! Abruptly, Michael asked, "Why didn't you have your headlights on?" The deputy replied, "Because I was observing the lightning in the storm that's coming up."

I sustained injuries to my shoulder and hip. An ambulance took me to the hospital. In the emergency room, I said to Michael, "Well, I guess we don't have to think about selling the Granada; the Sheriff's Department just bought it." I did not have any broken bones. The doctor loaded me up with 800 mg. tablets of Ibuprofen and discharged me from the hospital the next day. However I returned forty-nine times for physical therapy during the next twenty-seven months.

After the accident, we went to the junkyard to look at the Granada. It was amazing. If we had collided a split second later, the other car would have hit my door and gone over or through the passenger area. After this, I wondered if I would live long enough to die of cancer. I could not understand how or why I knew the accident would happen. It seemed similar to the premonition of Les's accident. I returned to the dictionary and found the word, telepathy. That is: communication of one mind with another, without using speech, hearing or sight. I did not like this word any better than premonition. Then I wondered who was communicating with me? And why? No one! No one could be communicating with me. That is not possible, and I still could not understand the force that pushed me to the doctor in February of 1986, that proved to extend my life. I could not understand any of this and I refused to think about it. I would bury it all in a little room and lock it tight. I decided I would never talk about it to anyone. I just wanted to live and be left alone.

The accident seemed a big step backward for my health. I swallowed bottles of painkillers and still felt lousy. Shoulder pain turned into headaches. Then my right eye throbbed. My hip ached when I walked, and sometimes when I sat. Physical therapy helped and finally I learned which exercises improved my condition.

*Now I Know Why*

The year 1988 ended on a downside for me. I met my friend, Betty, in the grocery store, and we visited for a while. We were close to the same age and had been involved in various activities together. Betty lived just two miles away. I heard she had surgery a few months earlier, and I asked how she was. I felt shocked when she replied, "My surgery was for ovarian cancer too. My doctor told me he got all the cancer. I feel just fine and I've gone back to work full time." A chill went down my spine. I stammered, "Isn't that weird? I thought ovarian cancer was rare. There has been two other cases of ovarian cancer besides us in the neighborhood." We decided it was just a coincidence and visited for a while longer. Betty certainly looked good and I wanted to feel confident that she would survive. Inside I began to feel uneasy and wondered who would be next.

The year 1989 presented me with many challenges. I changed my career from in-home assistance with handicapped people to working at a center for mentally and physically handicapped people. Beginning part-time, made it easier to schedule my endless physical therapy treatments and doctors' appointments.

Feeling optimistic, my medical problems would resolve themselves I decided to work some extra days. If that went well, I would begin to work full-time. Reality hit hard and fast. Fatigue hit me much harder than I expected. A simple case of the flu put me right back in the hospital. The white cell count in my blood had not returned to normal after the

*Audre Kramer*

chemotherapy. I had half as many as I should have. Still struggling with my accident injuries, the headaches were harder to deal with on a full-time basis. I would have to be satisfied working part-time. On the other hand, part-time seemed much better than not working at all.

## *Chapter 10*

# QUESTIONS WITHOUT ANSWERS

One evening while watching television, I became frustrated with the fuzzy reception. I grumbled and changed channels while Mike stated that the television looked fine to him. Oh well, maybe I was just tired.

Then I realized other things did not look right either. Laundry did not look white after I washed it and reading seemed difficult. But this could not be, I just had my eyes checked by the ophthalmologist. He felt my eyes had recovered considerably from the chemotherapy. However, he reminded me in the long term, he did not know what to expect.

Feeling I could not face more medical problems, especially blindness, I decided to wait a while. Maybe I just needed to rest my eyes more often. That did not help. Each week I could see a little less. I would have to go back to the doctor. Maybe there would be something that could reverse this. I really dreaded the appointment.

I tried to focus on my struggles so far. The road had been bumpy, but considering that others with my diagnosis had struggled and died, I decided I could handle whatever news my doctor gave me.

My doctor didn't expect to see me back so soon. After an extensive examination he announced, "You have cataracts in both eyes." He seemed puzzled by this and said, "Do you have other family members with cataracts?" I replied, "My father and grandmother developed cataracts in their seventies." He said, "You are quite a bit younger, but it can happen. Maybe the chemo caused more trauma than we thought. You will need an operation on each eye to correct this." I frowned and said, "That will make five operations in less than four years. As much as I hate the thought of more surgery, I am anxious to get my eyesight back." He comforted me by saying, "Cataract surgery has advanced in the last years, and the outcome is usually good."

I clung to that thought before each operation when they injected each eye with five shots of Novocain. Prior to 1986, shots never bothered me. But now after over a hundred I became quite squeamish. These ten injections seemed nearly more than I could stand.

My eye surgery succeeded and my vision was actually better than before. Each implant contained some correction. I still needed glasses but now they were not so thick. I felt really upbeat and strong. Each day that went by reduced the odds that my cancer would return.

My jubilation didn't last long. Katherine, another member of our small church, was diagnosed with ovarian cancer. She lived two miles away. Her surgeon told her that she had a good chance to survive. She looked so good I wanted to believe it. However, they told Alice that she was cured and now she was gone. They told Betty two years ago that they removed all of the cancer and now she was gravely ill. A few months later (March 1990) Betty died. This disease showed no mercy. If you get it, you die!

Earlier events began to plague me. How and why did I know that my brother would have that terrible accident in 1978? Why was I compelled to see a doctor in 1986 to detect my cancer early, when my friends are dying of the same disease? How and why did I know about my own accident in 1988 before it occurred? These things just do not happen; at least not to anyone I know.

When I was a child, I thought it would be great to know the future. I could tell farmers what the weather would be so they would know what to plant. I could predict the stock market and make a lot of money to feed hungry people. I could predict a crime and save someone's life. But this is not the way it is working out. I had some forewarning about my brother's accident, but not the date or location. The forewarning proved useless to save his life. There is no greater pain than to know what will happen and not be able to change the outcome. This is not the way it is supposed to be. WHY, WHY, WHY did I have to know what would be next? Then it happened again!

## Chapter 11

# MY SHARED NEAR DEATH EXPERIENCE

Exhausted, I settled down to watch television alone one evening in the spring of 1990. Little did I know that the next hour would change my life forever! I switched on the television to watch one of my favorite shows, Unsolved Mysteries. It was scheduled to profile two cases of near death experience. I saw a program a few years earlier dealing with this subject, and found it to be an interesting theory.

Simultaneously, when the show aired, I was taken by the hand and led on a most joyful experience. It seemed similar to my earlier experience when someone took hold of me and led me to the doctor ahead of time. This time I was led through someone else's NDE; much like a lesson in which I was being taught. Information by-passed my five senses and imprinted firmly in my mind. As the people were interviewed and reliving their experiences, I was there with them. Yet, I know I never left my chair. As they passed through the tunnel and into the light (HEAVEN), I could see past what was on the screen. I received brief flashes of the

*Now I Know Why*

LOVE and PEACE that is there. It felt addictive, and I constantly crave for more (each night when I fall asleep, the memory returns). It seemed overwhelming! Words like majestic, breathtaking, beautiful, or glorious are just not appropriate. The words have not been made that can describe this. It felt like God laying his hand on my cheek and saying, "HEAVEN IS REAL AND I AM THERE WAITING FOR YOU."

I could feel what they described when they observed their life review (viewing one's life from beginning to end and feeling all the pain and pleasure caused to others). I was not aware of stepping out of this world and into that one. However, when the program ended, returning to this world felt like having a pail of ice water dumped on me. The whole thing seemed so typical of all my earlier experiences. I received enough information, clearly and decisively, to know what would happen; but never given as much information as I wanted or thought that I needed.

Shortly before I lamented because I was forced to know what would be next. Now, knowing what would be next was the greatest gift I could receive. My earlier Catholic background taught me that God was a vengeful God, always waiting to send me to hell if I did something wrong. Now I knew that was not true. God is great love! He is always waiting for me to repent and return to his loving embrace. It felt so good! It felt like some sort of super high!

*Audre Kramer*

I just could not process all of this. It was too much at one time. I always hoped that heaven was real. Now I knew for sure. Dying no longer seemed one bit frightening. I wanted to tell everyone, yet I knew I could tell no one. How could I make anyone understand? Like the earlier events, I would have to put it all in my secret room and close the door tightly, lest all of the events would come flying out. I just could not deal with that. No one would ever believe me, and I never wanted to discuss the premonition of Les's accident. It always made me feel like crying, and I do not do that.

I reasoned this is my gift; God gave it to me. I decided never to talk about these events even if someone nailed me to the floor. Before this incident, I didn't know the source of my premonitions and telepathy. I could not be sure some evil force was not toying with my life. Now I

*Now I Know Why*

knew the source. It was God. I felt relieved and so happy I could hardly stand it.

*   *   *

Amid my physical therapy treatments and many doctor appointments, I needed to see my dentist. My teeth were fracturing at an alarming rate. When the dentist removed a filling, the remainder of the tooth would crumble. He did not know what to make of it. We concluded it was just one more complication from the trauma I had been through. Of course this meant a multitude of Novocain shots. It seemed I would never get away from needles. Thank God for crowns.

Our neighbors, Doug and Joyce were building a beautiful log cabin. We enjoyed watching it go up and shared their enthusiasm. Each time we drove by we admired it a little more. Occasionally we stopped in, and Doug would give us a tour of the latest construction. Soon after completion, we learned that Doug had been diagnosed with colon cancer. Colon cancer is like ovarian cancer in that it usually has spread by the time it is discovered. This seemed the case with Doug.

My doctor appointments and my job kept me so busy that I did not get to visit with Doug until several months later. He came over, and I would be gone, or I went there, and he would be gone. Finally, we met in our oncologist's waiting room and vowed we would get together to discuss our cases. Two days later Doug came over. Our visit lasted three hours. He looked good but appeared extremely overwrought. He asked my opinion about future treatment. I told him I would give it a try. He could always stop if it proved too harsh. Basically he looked strong. Maybe there would be another miracle. After all, I made it over two years now, and that was certainly a miracle. As we discussed our situation, it became clear that fear was destroying Doug faster than the cancer. He confided he could not sleep, and his life seemed consumed by what may lie ahead. I knew how he felt.

Doug wanted to talk to someone other than a family member. He sought me out because we shared the same situation. He wanted to know how I coped with having this disease. More importantly, he wanted to know how I would cope with dying from this disease. I hesitated for a minute. Could I share my secret with Doug? How much should I tell him? Before I could think about it I blurted out, "Have you ever heard of Near Death Experience?" He said he had not, but he seemed curious. I described it in general terms and told him that I had some personal experience with it. I did not go into detail. I asked him if he would like to read some articles about it, and he said he would. Oh, how I wished I had taped the program that profiled the NDE cases.

The following day I went to the library and found four good articles. I took them to Doug, and he studied them over. It became clear that it made a positive impact on his state of mind.

Shortly thereafter, another popular program (20/20) aired a segment on NDE. Then the original program in which I had taken part reran their segment. I taped both. This presented a unique opportunity for me to study the program without the addition of my NDE. So much was different. So much was missing. This time it was just pictures on the screen. The producer's attempt to display God's light and the radiant colors seemed almost feeble. Most important, this time I was alone and not being led by the hand. The feeling of love and peace was absent. However, it was still an excellent program, and I will cherish the tape forever.

A few days later, a popular talk show interviewed several people who had NDES. I taped that show as well and gave all the tapes to Doug. He kept them several weeks and watched them over and over again. When he returned the tape to me, I sensed a feeling of peace that had not been there before. During the months to come we shared a special friendship. The future for both of us would be a constant struggle.

My cancer check-ups constantly reminded me of my fragile existence. I failed them for one reason or another. Once my doctor felt a mass in my stomach. Further testing resolved that. Then my pancreas became enlarged. Further tests revealed cancer was not present. In August of 1990 I failed my check-up, big time. My oncologist discovered a serious lump in my breast. There was a high probability of cancer. My oncologist discussed some options with me. Remove the lump only or remove both breasts to lower my future cancer risk. I went to a surgeon for another opinion. He seemed familiar with my past history, but came to a different conclusion. He believed the lump was not cancer and removing it would be adequate. After more tests and conferences ten days passed. It seemed like ten years. I tried to prepare for all possibilities: dying of breast cancer, losing both breasts or could I be lucky enough to get by with just a lumpectomy?

Finally a decision arrived. Remove the lump, test it and the surrounding tissue, and evaluate the results. If the lump were cancer, we would remove both breasts and consider implants. I hated to think of any of it.

I really needed some good news, and I got it. The lump was not cancer, and other tissue samples were favorable. What a relief! There was a down side though. This constant battle of trying to survive was wearing me down.

The end of 1990 brought more bad news. JoAnn, another member of our small church, was diagnosed with ovarian cancer. She lived two miles away. I felt dumbfounded. She was the sixth victim with ovarian cancer in our small rural community. Ovarian cancer is not that common. How could this be?

*Chapter 12*

# BACK TO HELL

F ebruary 1991 was a day I had been waiting for. That is the magic five-year anniversary which all cancer sufferers celebrate. If you are cancer free that long, you are considered cured. I reached that goal to learn my doctor changed my celebration date to ten years. I soon learned all the life insurance companies agreed. I still could not obtain coverage. Oh well, at least I did not feel sick and things were going fairly well.

I kept myself occupied learning to handle my pain problems from the car accident. As an outpatient at Abbott Hospital's pain center, I would be there for several days at a time and return home for the weekends. Disliking big cities I looked forward to getting back.

Our Sundays consisted of the usual pattern; church, brunch and outdoor activity with the family. By mid-afternoon my stomach felt uncomfortable, but I kept up with the others. At supper I felt too uncomfortable to eat more than a single bite and a swallow of lemonade. Within minutes I felt considerable pain and decided to lie down for a while. Soon I felt nauseated and stumbled to the bathroom. Unable to stand, I slipped to the floor. After resting several minutes I crawled back to my bed and assessed my condition. In an hour's time I had become nauseated, experienced severe stomach pain and could not stand up. I begged, "God help me, I'm really sick." My bedroom was at the far end of the house and Mike and Mark were watching TV at the other end of the house. I rested for a minute and gathered enough strength to call out for help. No answer! Both televisions were on; one in the basement, the other in the living room. I would have to yell louder for my voice to carry over all the noise. Resting again I took a deep breath (oh, how that hurt) and called out again. This time I got a response. My son, Mark came into the room. He said, "What's the matter Mom?" I replied, "I am really sick, get Daddy!" A second later Mike was in the room. Excitedly he said, "What's the matter?" I replied, "I'm in a lot of trouble here, my stomach is killing me. I need to get to the hospital." Hurriedly we made the necessary preparations. Mike decided he would ask our long time friend and neighbor, Marge, to accompany us. The hospital was thirty-five miles away, and he did not want to be alone in the waiting room again.

We traveled only a few miles when things got much worse. The pain seemed unbearable and I felt myself slipping into a more critical situation. I groaned, "I need an ambulance. Can you get to a phone?" Mike replied, "It's Sunday night, everything is closed. Maybe something will be open in the next town." Then a little miracle occurred. Just ahead he saw flashing lights. A patrol car had pulled over another vehicle. Mike anxiously said, "Hey, maybe we could get a police escort or something." He ran over to the patrol car and returned with a plan. "They won't give us an escort, but they are sending an ambulance to meet us." The patrolman said we could not exceed the speed limit, even in an emergency, and we did not, until we were out of his sight. We turned on our flashers so the ambulance would recognize our vehicle when we met.

Shortly thereafter the transition was complete. The ambulance sped through the cold February night. I could hear the attendants discussing my condition with their headquarters. They started an I.V. and asked a few simple questions to help evaluate my condition. When they asked my name and what day it was, I managed to answer. Other simple questions like, who is the president, etc., were difficult to answer. Concentration seemed non-existent. I just wanted the pain to stop. Off in the distance, I could hear the sound of the surgeons sharpening their knives - - - - - again.

In the flurry of emergency room procedure they asked more questions I could not answer. "What did you eat? How long have you been sick? Have you ever had this before? What is that scar on your stomach from?" Good thing I was not alone.

Another small miracle, the emergency room doctor was a gastrointestinal specialist. Such luck on a Sunday evening, but his instructions didn't thrill me. He told the nurses not to administer pain medication until he reached a diagnosis." They pulled up the sides of the gurney so I would not roll off as my body jerked around from the pain. I ground my teeth big time, again. Blood tests and x-rays were ordered. All came back appearing to be normal. I couldn't tell them my white blood count is abnormally low. Therefore, when it began to climb it appeared to be in the normal range. Hours dragged by. Another small miracle, my surgeon was already at the hospital with another patient. A conference was ordered, then another examination by the surgeon. Hours passed with unbearable pain. They agreed a nasogastric tube should be put in place. Even though in terrible mental and physical condition, I remembered the nasogastric tube from before!

A large tube big enough to pull up undigested food is threaded through the nose, down the throat and into the stomach. Getting it down is nothing short of torture. I actually had to swallow the tube or it would not go down. They gave me water to drink while inserting the tube in an effort to force me to swallow. I did. But the water caused me to vomit which is miserable to do with a tube down my throat. At this point I would have cut any deal to get away from the pain. Death would have been a welcome visitor.

A decision needed to be reached. Time dragged by and I got weaker by the minute. Without any abnormal tests to back them up, physicians are slow to operate. The options were: administer pain medication and wait until the next morning to do a CT-scan or operate late on a Sunday night.

After six long hours of relentless pain the decision was made. It would be too risky to wait until morning. They would operate now. Their decision was correct. Surgery revealed a strangled bowel caused by adhesions. In that six hour period of time part of my bowel turned black and died. I lost approximately one foot of bowel during the course of the resection. Thank God they did not wait until morning. Not much of my bowel would have been left. Gangrene would have been my fate.

*Now I Know Why*

While recovering, I spent many hours sitting in my precious bay window. It seemed the perfect place to reflect on my latest brush with death. I felt both happy and sad. Happy that I did not have to know in advance that this would happen. Sad that I still did not have a traditional NDE like some other people. It seemed there were many tiny miracles in place to prevent it, this time.

In the following months it seemed like the little room that stored my experiences became too small. Something had to give. I felt relieved that so much had been written and broadcast about NDE. It gave me the courage to admit that I had a NDE, though I never described it in detail.

I decided to lend my tapes to my family and friends in hope that they would understand NDE well enough for me to describe mine. After viewing the tapes, my friend Bonnie gave me the best definition of NDE I had ever heard. She said, "NDE's are simply modern day miracles." I am sure she is right. It has been nearly 2000 years since Jesus walked this earth. We humans have a short memory. NDE serves to remind us of his heavenly promise.

*　　*　　*

Through the years Perry and Paige maintained contact with some of Ron's family. They learned Ron's relative, Julie (the person interviewed for my annulment), suffered from cancer and seemed quite ill.

I wanted to visit her but felt concerned about the secret we shared. Fifteen years had passed since the annulment. I decided a simple visit should be safe enough.

I called Julie to see if she felt up to a visit. She stated that she did and seemed pleased at my request. We set a date and a few days later we got together. Julie seemed surprised when I told her I had cancer, too. We discussed our treatment. It became clear Julie struggled with her disease; being a strong person she maintained a positive outlook. We discussed many things. Julie expressed concern about my children's lives. It felt good to know she still cared. I told her of the positive impact the annulment had on our lives. Shortly thereafter it came time to leave and I needed to tell her one more thing. She smiled when I said, "Thank you. Thank you. Thank God for you."

A few months later Julie died. Paige and I attended the funeral and kept a low profile. Although happy Julie no longer suffered, and could enjoy heaven, I felt sad the circumstances of our lives had put a great distance between us.

Early in 1992, my friend Doug became seriously ill. We visited regularly between his trips to Texas where he received the latest experimental treatment. As I drove past his log cabin one afternoon, I remembered he was due to leave again. I turned around and went back. I am glad I did. Doug sat in the living room looking extremely weak and thin. He had not eaten for quite awhile. His wife Joyce, had nearly finished packing, and then they planned to leave. As we visited it became

*Now I Know Why*

clear that just talking tired him greatly. When Joyce finished it was time for us to leave. Doug struggled to stand up and we slowly walked to the door. I gave him a hug and told him, "Good-bye." It was hard to leave him that day; I knew I would never see him again.

Doug lingered awhile longer and died in March. I felt sad since I would miss him greatly. Several weeks later I drove past the cabin again and marveled at his beautiful tulips. It reminded me he was in heaven, a place of great beauty and peace. As I drive past the cabin now, I suspect there might be one more log cabin in heaven.

Days of struggle lay ahead. Katherine, JoAnn and I were the only survivors left of the six ovarian cases in the neighborhood. Katherine still held her own. JoAnn continued to do well. However, I was in trouble again. My vision began to grow dim once more. It seemed like blindness loomed over me like a flock of vultures waiting to pluck out my eyes. Oh how I hated to go back to the ophthalmologist. What if he could not fix it this time? I made the appointment and forced myself into his office. Fortunately, it was reversible again. Scar tissue from the cataract surgery had grown across my eyes causing my vision to be comparable to looking through a curtain.

Thank God for lasers. A couple of blasts in each eye blew the scar tissue to bits. That was quite a light show! The best part was it did not hurt. In a few hours when the eye drops wore off, I could actually see clearly again.

*Audre Kramer*

Summer (1992) drew to an end. Katherine lost her battle and died in August. That left JoAnn and me. At least she seemed to be doing all right, and there were no new cases of cancer in the neighborhood. Maybe we were the last of the ovarian plague in this tiny community.

*Chapter 13*

# ENLIGHTENING HISTORY

In 1993, I looked back over the previous seven years, and it had a profound effect on me. I had cancer, seven operations, chemotherapy and a car accident. I came to realize survival comes at a high price, both physically and mentally.

I developed some strong feelings about what I would allow medically in the event of another terminal illness. Researching living wills and D.N.R. (Do Not Resuscitate) statements I decided both were appropriate for me. It is one thing to be acutely ill with the possibility of getting well. It is quite another to be terminally ill and knowing you cannot get well. I decided the ONE who started my heart, should be the ONE who stops it. I felt comfortable putting all my trust in God.

At the same time, I decided as long as I am on this earth, I wanted to be as healthy as possible. I would have to find a way to strengthen my immune system, intestinal tract, hip and shoulder and try to build some endurance. I made several attempts at an exercise program since I got sick, but each time I would get knocked down by another operation. Each time it seemed harder to get back up.

I decided on walking and riding bicycle. These were activities I enjoyed before having cancer. At times the difficulty of getting from my bed to the sanctuary of the bay window discouraged me, but each day went a little better. During the first ten minutes it seemed difficult to keep going, but then I actually felt better. After two years I could walk four miles in one hour. Then I needed a little nap. I did this three times a week.

After researching nutrition, I added small amounts of a wide variety of vitamins and minerals and healthful food to my diet. I surmised I must be here for a reason. Whatever it is, I want to do it well.

In the middle of 1993 I had an opportunity to visit with my favorite aunt, Delores. Actually, she seems more like an older sister. I felt comfortable admitting to her that I had a NDE. It surprised me to learn she also had a NDE. Not only that, but her mother (my grandmother) had three. Suddenly, I did not feel so unusual. That felt wonderful!

She willingly shared her experience with me. The following is an account of aunt Delores's NDE:

> "In the spring of 1962, I had an appointment with an oral surgeon to have an impacted wisdom tooth taken out. I was put to sleep for what should have been a thirty-minute surgery. While asleep, I had a wonderful experience. I found myself walking

*Now I Know Why*

along a grassy field with a stream running close by. It was so clean and bright! I saw everything in vivid color and detail. But most of all, I felt a happiness and peace I had never experienced. I wanted to stay there forever. I knew I had to leave and come back, but I didn't want to.

When I woke up in the dentist's chair, I was hemorrhaging from my mouth. Blood streamed down my chin into a pan. The nurse held my head, and the dentist told me he was going to burn the artery he severed during the extraction. The "thirty minute surgery" lasted almost two hours. When I think about what happened and close my eyes, I can almost see that place. But I can't recapture the feeling I had there."

The following is an account of my grandmother's three experiences as told to me by Aunt Delores:

"When my mother was three months pregnant with her ninth child (of thirteen children), she had an emergency appendectomy. In 1921 this was a life threatening procedure. During the surgery she saw a beautiful lady standing above her in the room. She smiled at Mother and she had a blue and white glow around her head. This is all she remembered when she woke-up."

"Another incident occurred to Mother during World War II. She had two sons in the service overseas. One son, my brother Clarence, was stationed in France and Germany. The other son, my brother Ervin, was a marine air corp pilot. During part of the pilot's maneuvers to different areas, Ervin was aboard a troop ship. He had to cross the equator as part of this journey. The custom on board was to initiate anyone in the service who had never crossed before. One day when Mother got up, she seemed very upset and worried. She was sure something happened to one of her sons. She seemed shaken and could hardly do her work. She cried several times. Months later, Ervin came home on leave and told about the terrible things that happened to him during the initiation. It was the exact day that Mother seemed so upset.

"Years later, Mother was caring for Ervin's children at his home. Ervin's wife was in the hospital after the birth of another child. He worked late into the evening to make extra money. Mother rested on the sofa waiting for Ervin to come home. It was around midnight when Ervin stood at the foot of the sofa and called her name. She got up and walked into the kitchen where the light had been left on, thinking he went in there. The room was empty. A little later she was notified that Ervin had been in a terrible car accident. He was critically injured and in a coma for three days."

Recently I had an opportunity to visit with Uncle Ervin, and I asked him what happened during his initiation when he crossed the equator. His initial reluctance to discuss the subject increased when I explained I was writing a book about my NDE, and told him his mother had some experiences involving him. This was news to Ervin since Grandmother shared her experiences with just a few people. Evidently she felt most people would not believe her; therefore, she was selective about whom she told. I know how she felt. After some coaxing, Uncle Ervin told me what happened that day.

"My squadron was on a troop ship, and some of us had never sailed across the equator before. We were separated from the others for the initiation. First they squirted us with fire hoses until the floor and all the men were soaking wet. Then they shocked us with electrical devices similar to cattle prods. Next they blindfolded us and made us drink whatever horrible concoctions they could mix together. Most of us vomited it right back up. Then they had a long canvas sleeve about twenty feet long and two or three feet in diameter. They made each man crawl through it. At the front of the sleeve there was a man with a fire hose aiming it into the sleeve, and in the rear there were men with paddles whaling on our backsides. One pilot came out of the sleeve swinging his fists, which turned out to be a big mistake. That pilot took quite a beating from the large group of men around us. We just had to take whatever they dished out. I would have to say that none of us were in danger of dying, but it was painful and extremely humiliating. Actually, we were in much greater danger from the enemy. We were on a large troop ship in the Pacific Ocean somewhere north of Australia and south of Hawaii. We sailed without any kind of escort. We were literally sitting ducks."

*Audre Kramer*

My grandmother lived to be ninety-six years old. I was thirty-five when she left us. How I wish I could talk to her again. She was a very special French lady. I remember her gazing at me one day and saying, "You know, when I was your age, my hair was just as dark as yours." She is part of my earliest memories. My grandparents lived across the road from us when I was a young child. I seemed to identify with her, and during my teen years I changed the spelling of my first name to the French version.

*Chapter 14*

# LEARNING "WHY"

After the flurry of television shows in 1990 and 1991, that detailed NDE, I began to feel frustrated and somewhat cheated. My NDE seemed a blessing, but I wanted to walk through the tunnel myself and be met by someone important to me. Maybe it would be Les. He could take my hand and walk one step ahead of me one more time. It would seem appropriate. I never had the chance to tell him "Good-bye."

I wanted to stand in God's light myself instead of standing in someone else's shadow. I wanted to stay there and absorb all the feelings of love and peace until I had my fill. Instead I got brief instances of that love and peace, kind of like someone else's leftovers.

I wanted my own "life review." That is: viewing one's life from beginning to end, and feeling all the pain and pleasure I caused others. I know my life review would not be great. After all, I made enough mistakes. But, I did some things right, too.

I wanted the chance to choose whether to stay there or return to this life. That choice would be easy. However it was not to be. I concluded God did not think I was worth an NDE of my own.

My experiences were so unusual I felt no one would believe me. So again, I decided to store the whole thing in my secret little room. But now it seemed like I stuffed too much in there. There was not enough room for all of it. I decided it would be safe to tell my family and friends that I had a NDE in the past, but I refused to describe it. That seemed to release some of the pressure. I hoped it would be enough.

When telling people about my NDE, I decided to say that mine differed from the traditional type. That part of mine (Les's death) was very painful to describe, therefore I would not do it.

Many times I did describe the 1986 incident when I was led to the doctor's office early for the cancer diagnosis. I told them I knew it was connected to my later NDE. They seemed to respect my decision not to go further.

This approach seemed to work all right for a year or so. Then I became increasingly troubled and frustrated, not able to understand why it was different. There were so many critical times since 1986 that a regular NDE could have occurred. The opportunities seemed endless. The times I stopped breathing, after the 1987 surgery, would have been a perfect opportunity, yet for some reason, it did not happen. Why, why, why did it have to be this way?

I could not see any value in putting myself through the misery of describing what happened. Again, I decided to try to forget the whole thing. This seemed too hard to understand. Besides, I wanted to concentrate on the gift of knowing for sure that heaven is real, and God is there. That always comforted me in the past. So why not keep that gift for myself and forget about everything else?

Alas, it just did not work. Something kept pushing me against my will. I did not know where to turn. Several times I thought of talking to a priest. However, I never heard one mention NDE during Sunday mass or any other time. After the trauma of dealing with my divorce and annulment, I did not want to risk being kicked out of the church again. Several months went by, and the problem didn't get better. Then I realized the solution might be right at hand.

We visited a counselor for one of my children who had a difficult adolescence. It seemed to me a counselor would have considerable exposure to NDE during his practice. After all, others might have felt a need to discuss their NDE with such a person.

I felt extremely hopeful. Perhaps he could help me process the past events so I could discover the reason for my non-traditional NDE.

As counselors go, this one seemed better than most. We did not always agree, but positive progress sometimes developed. He was Catholic like we were, not that it should matter since NDE is non-denominational.

I decided, before discussing this with him, to screen him to determine if he would be helpful in this matter. At the end of our next session, I stayed in the room after the others left. I began by asking if he or a member of his family or close friend ever had a NDE. He said, "No." I asked him if he ever counseled anyone who did? He replied he had not. Then I asked if he could define NDE? He replied he knew what it was, but his definition seemed vague, and he stumbled badly. It became clear he would not be helpful with the situation.

More discouraged than ever, I asked God, "Why did this happen to me? Why was my NDE different? Traditional NDE works so well. Why did you change it?" To say, "God works in mysterious ways," is an understatement. I just wanted to be like everyone else. I became angry with God. This did not make any sense, and I did not understand it. I thought, "God, you must have me mixed up with someone else."

Clearly, no one was out there to help me, and I would have to walk this road alone.

I realized, in God's eyes, I must be sounding like a spoiled brat. I needed to calm down and think more rationally. I decided to pray about this, and hope understanding and meaning would be sent to me. After all, it happened before.

Deciding to go back to my collection of taped interviews I watched them again. Maybe there was something I missed. There had to be an answer somewhere. Sure enough, it was right in front of me, yet I never realized it until then. My non-traditional NDE did have a purpose after all.

After the interviews, in every case, a skeptic from the scientific or medical profession would be interviewed to explain why NDE is not real. They contend NDE is a neurological condition that occurs when the brain shuts down and suffers from lack of oxygen. Or NDE is the result of medication that can cause hallucinations. Other times, they say NDE is merely wishful thinking or dreams that are slanted by religious beliefs.

I am an example in which none of the above is the case. During the incidents I experienced, there were never any medications involved. The most significant thing about the times I stopped breathing and suffered from lack of oxygen was that, it was so very insignificant. Nothing happened. As far as dreams are concerned, I was always awake when these incidents occurred. I cannot deny I was taught there is a God. And by now, he must be saying, "You catch on pretty slow."

I heard those arguments so many times before, but never applied them to my situation. I know 'me' pretty well. If I had a traditional NDE, I would not have revealed the other incidents because I desperately wanted to be like all the others. The skeptics would go on saying NDE is not real, and I know most will continue to do that. My non-traditional NDE did have a purpose. Maybe God does consider me worthwhile. I realize now, no matter how many times I might stop breathing, I will probably never have a traditional NDE. Maybe that is all right. Considering the trauma my body has already been through, I doubt it will be too long before I walk through that tunnel and stand in that light forever. After this insight, I began to feel more comfortable with what happened.

Sometime later, while paging through a magazine, I saw an ad for a statue of Jesus with two children. One child sat on his lap, the other leaned against his knee. The loving expression on Jesus' face immediately brought back the feelings of my NDE. I clipped out the ad and tucked it away, hoping someday I could afford to buy the statue.

A few months later, I heard about a popular book dealing with an extensive NDE. I decided to read it and called the library to see if they had it. To my dismay, I learned there was a long waiting list. Anxious to read the book, I decided to buy it instead. When I purchased the book, the sales clerk commented to a co-worker, "This is the last copy, again. We just can't keep it on the shelves."

I was delighted with the book. As I read it, I could hardly wait to get to the next page. It felt great to know many people would be exposed to NDE by this book's popularity. I discovered other recently published books on NDE and found them interesting as well. It comforted me to know other people had the courage to disclose what had happened to them. Deep down, I began to feel I would never have any peace unless I revealed what happened to me. It would be far too complicated and painful to ever explain verbally, but I knew I could write it.

The problem with that is, I do not like to write. I am not great on reading either. I enjoy researching science and medicine but not much else. Writing my experiences would be a huge undertaking. It would take a lot of time, and I already had my time filled with my family, two elderly parents and a part-time job. Writing needs to be done indoors in this climate and I like to be outdoors. This was not going to be fun.

I decided to start collecting my medical records. If they were not still available, I would not even begin to write. One doctor had died and another retired. Surprisingly, I did find nearly all of the records. That put the pencil in my hand.

I began with an outline and found that to be time consuming. I had to remember things I'd worked very hard to forget. I began to drag my feet. This seemed just too hard to do. I just could not find the right words to describe what I needed to say.

Much to my surprise I would get a little boost from somewhere at the oddest times. I would be driving, walking or working, and all at once the words were there. I needed to write them immediately or I would seem to lose them. Frequently, while driving I pulled over and stopped to make a few notes. Most annoying, I awoke in the middle of the night and sentences would start to pour in. I had to get up and write quickly, then try to fall back to sleep. Over a period of time this multitude of notes turned into pages of my book. I struggled on.

*Audre Kramer*

## Chapter 15

# JOANN'S STORY

The spring of 1994 seemed an exciting time. Two years earlier our daughter, Paige, married a fine young man named Michael. That made two Michaels in the family. Now Paige and Michael presented us with our second grandchild. They named her Tessa, and she is such a joy. It had been seven years since we had a baby in the family. It was so much fun to watch my daughter become a mother. So much fun to watch Michael bestow endless kisses on Tessa's tiny forehead. So much fun to observe my two granddaughters relate to each other. These joyous, precious moments in my life gave me strength to face the months that lay ahead.

Midsummer brought a painful reminder of my struggle with cancer. JoAnn, my friend and only other survivor in the group of six, suffered her third recurrence after several years of health. I felt certain she had beaten her cancer. "She has to get well", I told myself, "I can't face losing her!"

*Now I Know Why*

I felt grateful the new drug, Taxol, had been found to fight ovarian cancer. Praying for her recovery, I waited for good news.

Good news never came. JoAnn, discouraged by the third recurrence, refused the surgery the doctors advised. She had enough. She set some definite limits on how much treatment she would accept. A few months later, she agreed to a colostomy when the tumor closed off her bowel. She also agreed to give Taxol a try. I prayed some more.

Things were not going well. By March of 1995, it was clear JoAnn was losing the battle. She stopped eating and received nourishment by I.V. only. She wanted to be at home instead of in a hospital. Necessary equipment was brought in and a public health nurse visited regularly.

Family and friends took turns at her side during the long days and nights. I desperately wanted to visit her. Maybe I could ease her struggle in some small way. When I called to set an appointment, it seemed difficult to arrange. Sometimes she would be having a bad day or be asleep. Other times the nurse would be there. Finally, there was a little space and I jumped at the chance. By this time most of the visits were short, fifteen minutes or so.

I arrived at 4:30 p.m. When I drove in the yard, not seeing any cars, I thought she probably went to the hospital. As I approached the front door, I saw a note that read, "come in". She was home! I felt glad, but a little surprised to see her alone. Her appearance surprised me even more. She sat in her recliner chair smoking a cigarette looking thin and frail. Tubes ran in and out of her body. Her hair was beginning to grow again, maybe a half-inch long. She smiled and said, "Hello." In an instant I knew it was the same ol' JoAnn. I could not believe how good she looked. She seemed sharp and alert and still had a twinkle in her eye.

We talked and talked. First, about her treatments and then her family. Then she asked if my book was finished. I regretted having to say no. She replied, "Well then, hurry up and finish it because I want to read it!" "I'll try," I told her "but I am really struggling with it."

She said, "You know, my father had a NDE shortly before he died." I replied, "Yes, I remember you telling me about it several years ago." We talked about it again, and I could see the impact it had on her. It seemed like a gift he gave her then, that became invaluable to her now. She seemed absolutely fearless concerning her own death. We talked about heaven and what it would be like.

With all the talking, JoAnn's throat seemed to get a little dry. She asked me to bring her a can of beer and a saltshaker. As she drank the beer we could see it exit through the drainage tube in her stomach. "Well, at least it tasted good for a little while," she said. We both laughed. I glanced at my watch and it was 5:50 p.m. I had been there for one hour and twenty minutes. I could not believe it had been that long. JoAnn barely seemed tired, though I knew she must be. As I prepared to leave, I told JoAnn I would return in a week or so. She replied, "Bring whatever you have finished on your book. I can't wait to read it." She was not prepared to take "no" for an answer.

As I drove home many thoughts went through my mind. I felt elated with our visit. She looked so much better than I expected. Yet, I knew she was dying. At the same time, I refused to accept losing her and I prayed, "JoAnn do not leave me here alone."

A few days later I became very ill with a nasty virus. My weakened immune system had a difficult time fighting it off. By the time I recovered, it was too late to visit JoAnn again. She died May 5, 1995.

JoAnn's death hit me hard. Six of us were thrown into this terrible situation and as each one died, part of me died too. Each time my world became a little smaller. I really needed JoAnn to survive with me. Now I felt terribly alone. I felt guilty. Why am I left here while they are there? I knew the "there" was heaven and they would not choose to return if they could. It did not console me to know that. I was separated from them, and I could not accept it.

When Alice, Eileen, Betty and Katherine died, I did not attend their funerals. Their disease and death mirrored my prognosis. That terrified me. I was a coward.

Instead, I showed up to work at their funeral luncheons if not too sick. Working there allowed me to take part in their funerals yet be safely away from viewing their tortured bodies. Assisting with their funeral luncheons was the last thing I could do for them.

I vowed I would break this pattern with JoAnn. I would attend her wake, funeral mass and work at her luncheon, too. I felt ready to accept the fact that JoAnn was in a better place, but breaking the bond between us proved more complicated.

The day of her funeral I thought I had everything under control. I felt comfortable knowing her suffering was over and only joy lay ahead for her. However, as I sat in our small country church, a problem developed for which I had not prepared.

*Audre Kramer*

The church was packed. The benches were full and people stood in the aisles and hallways. JoAnn had many friends. As I scanned the crowd, it became difficult to watch them. Their grief was terrible to see. Feeling prepared to see her family's pain, I discovered I was not prepared to observe one of her best friends. The anguish on her face and the tears said it all. My heart was breaking and I cried buckets of tears—on the inside.

As the procession left the church, I observed the family members file past me. One of JoAnn's daughters, Tammy, seemed to have a peaceful strength about her. She held her father's arm in a comforting manner that baffled me.

I went to the dining hall to work as the crowd proceeded to the cemetery. I tried unsuccessfully to regain my perspective as I served the luncheon. It seemed impossible to break that bond and let her go.

When the luncheon ended, I was cleaning in the kitchen when Tammy found me. She had a glow about her face I could not understand. She began, "I have to tell you, my mom had a vision or something before she died. She told us after your visit that you had a NDE, too. I wish I had time to talk to you, but I have to leave with my family." I replied, "I want to talk to you, too. We will have to get together soon. Write down everything you can remember about it." That glow in Tammy's face helped me regain my perspective and a sense of peace came over me.

Tammy is JoAnn's middle daughter. Terri is older and Trisha is younger. I knew Tammy the best because she was a student in my religion class seventeen years earlier.

During Memorial Day weekend, Terri, Tammy, Trisha and I had a chance to visit. They were remarkable. They were excited and all wanted to speak at the same time. I got out my note pad and began to write. The following is their account of the experience they shared with their mother the night before she died.

May 3, 1995: JoAnn lapsed into a semi-conscious state. She seemed comfortable and in her own little world. She had busy hand movements like eating but there was nothing in her hands.

May 4, 1995, JoAnn's condition worsened and she lapsed into a coma. Her family gathered, including her brother, Bud. (He seemed very protective during JoAnn's early life and continued to have a close relationship with her.) Bud was present until 8:30 p.m. At midnight the family dispersed to the following areas:

JoAnn was lying in her recliner chair;

Cletus (JoAnn's husband) was asleep on the sofa;

Trisha and Tammy were sleeping upstairs, and

Terri was at JoAnn's side.

JoAnn began to speak. She did not look at anyone in the room.

JoAnn asked for EILEEN. Eileen is JoAnn's cousin who cared for JoAnn's mother in a nursing home. Eileen was present when Joann's mother died and stayed until her body was removed from the room.

JoAnn stated, "ONE IS BAPTIZED AND THREE WILL BE." This referred to Tammy's children. One was baptized and three were not. (The process has since begun.)

JoAnn stated, "I HAVE NOT SEEN MY MOTHER YET."

JoAnn stated, "I FOUND MY LITTLE BROTHER." This referred to a stillborn baby brother.

2:30 a.m. Tammy came downstairs and stood near her mother's head. She began praying the Lord's Prayer in her mind. Half way through the third Lord's Prayer, JoAnn picked up the prayer exactly where Tammy was and finished it.

2:50 a.m. JoAnn stated, "I AM DYING."

Trisha came downstairs.

JoAnn began to ask for more time. "JUST ANOTHER HALF HOUR." During the next few hours she repeatedly stated, "JUST A FEW MORE MINUTES."

JoAnn repeatedly asked for "BUD."

JoAnn stated, "OH, SO THERE IS A GOD. WILL I KNOW ANYONE THERE?"

JoAnn seemed troubled by forgiveness and stated, "I CAN NOT FORGIVE THEM. I DO NOT CARE." We do not know whom she meant.

JoAnn asked for "BUD." Then stated, "BUD, LIFT ME UP."

6:30 a.m. Tammy left the home and went for a short drive.

Eileen arrived.

JoAnn stated, "EILEEN IS HERE TO HELP. YOU ARE HERE NOW."

Tammy returned and entered the driveway. JoAnn was not in a position to see this. She stated, "THEY ARE ALL HERE NOW."

8:00 a.m. The nurse arrived. JoAnn seemed restless and in pain. The decision was made to use painkillers, against JoAnn's earlier wishes. Ativan and morphine were administered. JoAnn seemed peaceful.

8:30 a.m. Bud arrived.

2:50 p.m. JoAnn left us.

Later, a member of the family reflected on these events. She summed it up best. "JoAnn paused in the doorway between this world and the next. She stood there long enough to give her family a special gift and carry on what seems to be a family tradition."

*Chapter 16*

# REFLECTIONS

As I begin this last chapter, I realize there is much to reflect on. Some things that I could not understand before are a little clearer now. When I researched the incidence of all cancers in our tiny community, I learned there was a definite increase in cancer in general. Besides the six ovarian cancers the following cases were diagnosed in the same time period.

                Josephine - lymphatic
                Les - prostate
                Freeman - skin
                Vivian - oral
                Fern - bone
                Doug - colon
                Wade - stomach

*Now I Know Why*

Carol - pancreatic

Cindy - breast

Virgil and Lorraine (husband and wife) - were both diagnosed with colon cancer in the same year.

Out of this group, Lorraine is the only survivor.

The three most common cancers in men are lung, prostate and colon. For women it is breast, colon and uterine. Ovarian is fifth. When you include six cases of ovarian cancer to the above group, the ratio is far out of proportion.

When I examined the years prior to 1984, it became easy to see the incidents of cancer rapidly increasing. After 1990, the cases began to decrease.

Now (1995), our community seems to have the average number of new cancers, and we pray the plague of earlier days does not return.

We will probably never know for sure what set off this plague, but I have developed a theory. A common factor we shared was our water. When I researched this theory, I found several incidents of contamination of our underground aquifer. I wondered how many incidents there were that I did not find.

Reflecting on the five incidents involved in my NDE:
1. 1977 - Les's accident - premonition;
2. 1986 - I was compelled to the doctor early, out of my control;
3. 1988 - my car accident - telepathy and premonition,

4. 1990 - my shared NDE - telepathy and premonition, possibly a type of vision.
5. 1994/95 - writing this book, something I never wanted to do.

The first four incidents can best be described as a door swinging open and information streaming out. The fifth resulted from the first four incidents. It seemed part of the package, so to speak. It became clear to me I must tell people what happened, and that I must do it the best I can.

The only incident I can prove is number two when I was led to a doctor I immensely disliked, which saved my life. I have the doctors' records that prove I sought medical attention without having symptoms, weeks ahead of my usual examination. Even the Pap smear, done two days before the surgery, came back normal.

When I reflect on my shared NDE, and the three incidents that occurred before it, one point becomes a little clearer. If just one or two of the events had been the extent of my experiences, I would have easily been able to "stuff it." It would have remained my secret forever. All of the events were necessary to force me to reveal what really happened. It has been a long journey, and I seemed to learn very slowly.

Sometimes when I think of the events of those years it all seems too much...it could not have happened. But then there are those constant reminders: I hear the siren of an ambulance and remember the night Les died. I walk into the church on Sunday morning and gaze at the cemetery seeing the graves of some of my partners who had the same type of cancer as I did. At night when I undress, I see the surgical scars on my body. But most of all, I am reminded when I feel that unrelenting craving for

*Now I Know Why*

that love I briefly tasted. Then I know it all did happen. Then I thank God because he carried me when I felt too weak to go on.

Now I hope the door that opened and allowed the information to flow to me will be closed. I know enough, now. Now I know why things happened the way they did. I have a blocking method which might prevent future information from passing through. It seems to work most of the time, though I definitely feel great pressure to accomplish certain things.

What if the next forewarning would involve losing my husband, a child, a grandchild, another brother or sister, or another close friend? I do not think I could stand that. I do not want to know these things in advance. Selfishly, I want my loved ones here because I am here. I realize as people grow old and sick it is best for them to move on. I can accept that. I find myself nagging my family and friends to have yearly checkups and to stop smoking if they are doing so. I want them to stay here until after I leave.

During the last several years, I have made contact with other people who also had NDE's. It is interesting how that works. During a conversation I may touch on the subject briefly. Some people respond immediately and tell of a family member who had a NDE. Others are more cautious. Later they may contact me and wish to discuss their own NDE privately. All seem to share a need to talk about their NDE and are concerned about being believed. Some become emotional and at some point begin to cry. I share that feeling. It is gratifying to see the relief they feel when they can finally talk about their experiences. A sense of peace seems to come over them.

Someone asked me, "How do you know these experiences aren't just daydreams?" I replied, "Daydreams occur every day. They are passive in nature and quickly forgotten. These experiences are profound, electrifying, emotional, and never forgotten. They occur before the incidents not after. The two are not even comparable."

When I reflect on my problem with crying, I have many feelings. Mostly, I am comfortable with crying on the inside. When that is difficult, I have a pretty good system. First, I flee from the situation. Then I refocus on what lies ahead (heaven). Then I remember, no one ever has to cry in heaven. A friend once told me Jesus wept. That thought has stayed with me. If it was all right for Jesus to cry, maybe someday it will be all right for me.

At some point, I became quite good at spotting phony "do-gooders". Some people have become quite wealthy as a result of their psychic abilities they attribute to God. I see many on television who cater to the rich and famous, and I remember Jesus was not wealthy and catered to the poor and helpless. Sometimes I wonder if their gifts are truly from God, or is it from some other source.

*Now I Know Why*

When we come to earth from heaven and are born, we are not allowed to remember the transition. Once here, we puzzle over where we will go when we leave. If we knew how wonderful heaven is, it might be difficult to stay here when we encounter life's struggles. Hence, it is hidden from us, as we each must complete our life's mission first.

As I reflect on my NDE, I realize it has motivated me to try harder to get to heaven. I have developed a "Where I Wanna Be" test. When I struggle between right and wrong, I just ask myself, where I wanna be? Then it is easier to do the right thing.

Sometimes it gets to be a real battle considering I am far from perfect. Then I remember, God made me, so he knows I cannot be perfect. I can only hope that someday when I meet him, he will say, "You did not do everything I asked, but you tried." When that happens, I know I will be all right.

Earlier, I stated I never read anything in my science and medical books that fit the description of my experiences. Now I realize I looked in the wrong place. There are many books by brave people who have come forward and revealed their NDE's. Also, the Bible has many prophets who knew of great future events. I know a little about what lies ahead but do not see myself as any kind of prophet. Biblical prophets were special people, and they were willing to reveal what they knew. I am nothing special and would rather not reveal anything.

*Audre Kramer*

While editing this book I grew more fearful that people would not believe my account of what had happened to me. Each day that went by made me feel more uncomfortable and soon I began to feel weighted down with a great burden. This was not what I really wanted to do, and I felt my writing skills were not adequate to do a good job. I had all the regular things in life to struggle with: a family, budgeting, a job, lack of time, etc. Now I had this book to worry about. I began to sink into a very deep low.

When Sunday rolled around I attended Mass as usual. As I sat in my pew I felt numb to my surroundings, and I hung my head in defeat. I decided to burn my book as soon as I got home. Suddenly, without warning, I received a blast of that "LOVE" I experienced during my shared NDE. It seemed even more intense than before and penetrated every cell in my body. It passed through me like a charge of electricity and delivered a feeling of warmth, wonder and beauty and again, more than I can describe. It lasted only a few brief seconds, but it was what I desperately needed. Then I understood. I should not worry if people do not believe me. I only need to write the best I can. Tears welled up in my eyes and I lifted my head and looked around. My little country church was filled with people and a glow surrounded them for a brief instant. Immediately, I was catapulted out of that terrible low and felt the strength I needed to go on.

The most difficult part of writing this book has been describing my NDE. I have put it off as long as possible but now will attempt to prepare you for what lies ahead. Come walk with me now and know what I expect when it is time to move on.

One day it will be my time to leave here. I will barely be aware of my leaving and may not realize I have left as I begin the journey. Probably I will be lying in a hospital bed and decide to visit a patient down the hall. Ahead I see a light far in the distance. At first it is a curiosity but very soon I will realize this is a light unlike any other. Wanting to move on there will be little concern about where I am going and even less about what I am leaving behind. All I can do is focus on the light and feel a tremendous desire to get closer.

Drawing nearer I am oblivious to everything and the light is all I see. It is beautiful and warm and loving and as I reach out I realize I am still along way from touching it. Struggling to move faster I realize I must get there any way I can.

Soon I realize someone is near me. Someone who knows me. Someone who loves me. Someone who will walk with me part of the way. I take their hand and continue toward the light. Now the light is brighter. I feel re-assured that I am safe, welcome and loved. But now something is happening.

Suddenly I realize the person who walked with me is gone. A vast panoramic view opens before me. I see myself as I lived my entire life. I see myself at all ages. I feel everything I ever felt. I am aware of everything I ever did. I feel all the pain I caused others. I feel all the comfort I gave to others. I understand that this is my life review. I understand that all will face a life review. I notice that when observing my life review I move closer to the light when I feel the comfort I brought to others. I move farther away from the light when I feel the pain I caused others. I understand that for those who have caused far more pain than comfort, they will step back from the light since they will not be able to withstand the pain they now must feel. They will fade away and I know not where they go.

Feeling the comfort I brought to others I step into the light and am given knowledge of all things. Now I understand all the things that happened in my life had a purpose. All the pain and struggle was there for a reason. There are no unanswered questions. When people treated me unfairly I understand what happened in their life that made them do the things they did. The harsh feelings I had about such incidents are gone. All I can feel is indescribable love. Love that far surpasses any love on earth. There is no feeling of want or desire as all is there before me.

There is still a part of the light that eludes me. I see the veil in front of me and want to move through it. I want to move on to what it is I have not seen. During my earlier NDE I was denied the vision behind the veil. Frozen in place I had to be content to wait until it is my time to stay. But this time I move forward. I see the vision behind veil is the face of God.

Upon closing this last chapter, I would like to share some observations I have made during this life.

If I could be granted one trivial wish, it would be to be able to sing. If I had a good voice, I would sing all day.

If I could be granted one serious wish, it would be to have some of the love that is in heaven, filter down through the clouds and fall onto the

*Now I Know Why*

earth like a gentle spring rain. That would solve all the problems on this earth.

I have complied a list of things in this world that I love and things in this world that I hate. The first list is the things that I love.

>My family;
>
>My friends;
>
>My little country church;
>
>Some solitude;
>
>Cool breeze on my face - summer;
>
>Warm bed - winter;
>
>Music, trees, flowers and agates;
>
>Watermelon, popcorn and chocolate;
>
>Frosty designs on my window on a cold winter morning;
>
>Wildlife at my feeders;
>
>Autumn, and;

Last, and most important, knowing that heaven is real and God is there.

The things in this world that I hate:

>War;
>
>Injustice and abuse;
>
>Dishonesty;
>
>Confrontations;

*Audre Kramer*

        Feeling cold;
        Putting my foot in my mouth;
        Snakes, skunks and flies;
        Needing to cry, and,
        Pain and feeling sick.

I had enough needles, steel stitches, scalpels, N-G tubes, vomiting, trips to the emergency room (eight) and ambulance rides. And I think, "God I do not like it here anymore. Please let me come home."

But then I look at the first list again and ponder the good that is there. I remember my mission here is not complete, and I realize I am not welcome there, early.

~~THE END~~

The best is yet to come.

## *About the Author*

Audre Kramer is the author of several published non-fiction short stories. She is the mother of three and grandmother of four. Her husband, Michael, is employed by a large dairy distributor in Minnesota.

After high school Audre was employed as a bookkeeper and later married. When her children were born she decided to put her career on hold and become a full time mom. After the children were grown she worked in the human services field with mentally ill people and later with mentally handicapped people. Presently she owns a small computer consulting service.

CPSIA information can be obtained
at www.ICGtesting.com
Printed in the USA
LVHW08s2150150718
583874LV00002B/126/P

9 780759 676763